FRET CUT RELIEF WORK

FRET CUT RELIEF WORK

THE ART & CRAFT OF
PAINTED RELIEF SCULPTURE

DAVID JONES

STOBART DAVIES
HERTFORD

British Library Cataloguing in Publication Data

A catalogue record for this book is available from the British Library.

ISBN 0–85442–069–X

Published 1997 by
Stobart Davies Ltd, Priory House, 2 Priory Street, Hertford SG14 1RN.

Set in $10\frac{1}{2}$ on $14\frac{1}{2}$ pt Ottawa by Ann Buchan (Typesetters) Shepperton.

Printed in Great Britain

CONTENTS

ACKNOWLEDGEMENTS

I would like to thank Roger Buse, who first suggested the idea of a book on fret cut relief work. Also my partner Jane Hulley, who read through the manuscript and gave much useful criticism, and to Brian Davies, for being such a friendly and helpful editor.

INTRODUCTION

The creation of images by relief carving is one of the earliest invented art forms and was practised in the Palaeolithic era at least as early as 30,000 BC. It was predominantly carried out in wood and stone and fine examples exist in every culture. Some that spring to mind are the huge stone mythical creatures of the Assyrian and Egyptian civilisations and the fantastic intertwined temple sculptures of India. The latter are sometimes so deeply carved as to be almost sculpture in the round.

The kind of relief carving to be dealt with in this book is on a somewhat more modest scale and uses modern and less labour intensive techniques.

It is a way of working I first evolved when I was putting together an exhibition of my wood sculptures. The gallery I was exhibiting in was all light oak and hessian. I realised that if I did not inject some colour in to the space my work would disappear in a haze of brown. I hit on the idea of making some large, bold, brightly painted reliefs to hang on the walls. They turned out to be the most popular items in the exhibition. I had found them very enjoyable to make as they combined two of my interests, painting and woodwork, in a stimulating way. The majority of my works since have been a continuing exploration of this technique.

In fret cut relief work there are three basic methods of creating the variation in surface levels that produce the relief effect. The first way is to draw the entire design out on a sheet of material and cut it out. Then by blocking up some pieces from behind with wood of different thickness a variety of levels are obtained. The second method is to use woods of different thickness to start with and to cut each piece to interlock with the next. Thirdly, the surface can be built up from above by gluing on pieces.

Each method has different advantages. For example, if everything is cut out of one sheet using a fine saw then each piece will fit together well with the next. Conversely, if the relief is constructed from various pieces of wood it is possible to exploit the natural colour and grain of the wood to enhance the composition. In practice more than one method may be used in any one picture.

The first part of the book deals with the tools and materials used to create fret cut reliefs. Methods of creating the work are discussed including painting and techniques for developing original designs. Particular attention is given in this section to ways of encouraging those who lack the confidence to produce their own drawings.

The second section of the book is a series of step by step projects, with suggestions to help the individual personalise them. Included in this part are examples of various works to inspire the reader to go on to create original and challenging projects of their own.

TOOLS

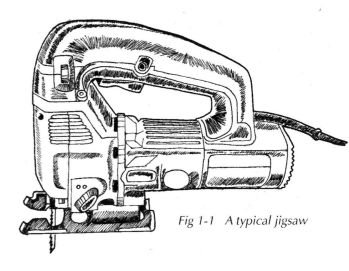

Fig 1-1   A typical jigsaw

Fret cut relief work can be produced using tools that are found in most tool boxes. A jigsaw, a sharp knife and something to hold the work are the minimum requirements.

The spectrum of what can be achieved is broadened with additional tools and I examine a range of them and their properties below.

TOOLS FOR CUTTING

The jigsaw

A variety of saws may be utilised to make fret cut reliefs. The saw with which I made my first pictures was a jigsaw and I still make use of it today.

The great advantage of a jigsaw is that there is no limit, except in thickness, to the size of material it can accommodate. The saw's drawback is that when cutting across or at an angle to the grain it tears the wood, even with the finest of blades. Some jigsaws have an insert which surrounds the blade that helps alleviate this problem. However it is quite difficult to see a line and follow it accurately when the attachment is fitted.

Fig 2-1   Typical damage to wood by a jigsaw cut. A: shows a cross cut. The grain is split on both sides of the cut. B: a diagonal cut. The grain is splintered on the side which is cut into. C: a ripping cut. The grain generally remains undamaged.

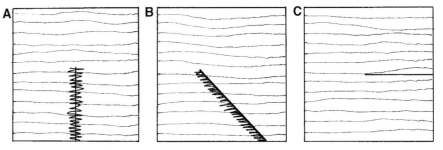

In the case of plywood in particular, the damage can be severe. If a lot of wood is to be carved away from the edge this may not matter. However, where the edge is important it is safest to draw the design in reverse on the back of the board and cut it from that side. It also helps, if the jigsaw has an orbital action, to set this very low or turn it off altogether.

You should use a thin fine toothed blade made for scroll sawing. For jigsaws such as the Bosch that use a cutter with a tag fixing, the T119BO blade is probably the best. It will cut wood up to 30 mm. thick.

Another problem with this type of saw is that when cutting hard or thick wood the cut may well not be square to the surface. When the blade has lost its edge this can be a real problem. Jigsaws also have limitations to their manoeuvrability, although this is not an issue for large scale work or where boldness of execution is an advantage.

Unless the design is simple the saw is not particularly good for pictures that are to be cut from one sheet. The blade removes too much wood, particularly on tight curves, so that when the pieces are reassembled, they do not fit together well.

One other thing to be aware of when using a jigsaw, as I know to my cost, is exactly what the saw is cutting. Make sure it's not sawing through the bench, floor or with intricate work, your fingers.

The fretsaw

The most versatile saw for relief work is probably the fret or scroll saw which can be either electric or treadle powered. This type of saw, if it has a parallel motion such as the Hegner uses, or another device that allows the blade to move with a perfectly vertical cutting action, is excellent. The saw will cut precise and intricate designs smaller than the structure of the wood can bear. I found on acquiring one of these saws, once I realised its potential, that I had to simplify what I was cutting out with it. The alternative was to be left with a collection of tiny, frail and unworkable pieces of wood that were an almost impossible puzzle to reassemble.

The saw cuts cleanly, requiring no further work to achieve a finished edge. The pieces fit back together well as so little wood is removed by the saw cut. The only real limitation of the machine is that the depth of its throat controls the length of cut that can be made in any one direction. However this can be overcome by careful design and if necessary the judicious use of a jigsaw for one or two crucial cuts.

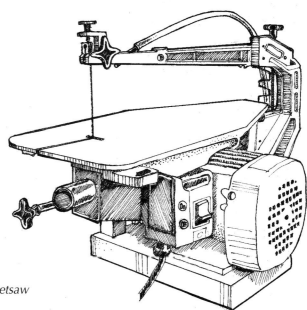

Fig 3-1   A typical electric fretsaw

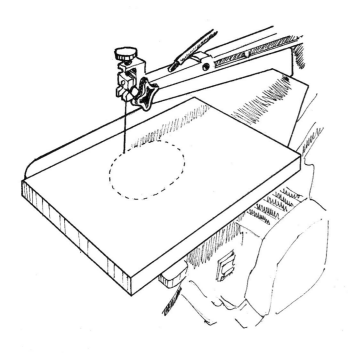

When cutting out something with a lot of pierced holes close together, such as a window frame with a lot of panes, it is possible to cheat and cut through from one hole to another. Provided the blade used is fine enough and the pattern of cuts well thought out, it will not notice in the finished work and it saves a considerable amount of time.

Fig 4-1 The piercing cut. If both pieces of wood are to be utilised, the hole drilled for the blade to pass through should be no bigger than the width of the saw blade.

Another advantage of the fretsaw is where piercing cuts have to be made. Because the blade is so thin only a very small hole needs to be drilled in the work. The blade is threaded through the hole and then re-mounted on the machine and the cut made. Both of the pieces of wood created can then be utilised.

Some saws have, or can be fitted with, a quick release knob on the top arm holding the blade. This can be very useful if a lot of piercing cuts have to be made as the blade does not need to be removed from the machine.

Fig 5-1 A good pattern of cuts to keep piercing to a minimum. First a piercing cut is made to remove the outer frame and panels. The inner panels are then removed following the dotted line. If a fine blade is used the cuts through the lattice can be glued with a drop of P.V.A. This method obviates the need for six piercing cuts. It would be particularly useful in a relief of a house with windows made of many small panes.

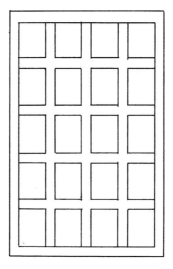

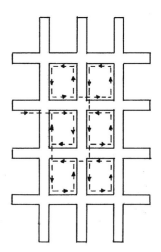

When using a fretsaw for fairly thin sections of wood, which is generally the case with relief work, only a small section of the blade is actually cutting the wood. It makes sense to make one or more wooden jigs to raise the table height to utilise more of the blade. I generally do the major cuts using the saw table and then cut up the smaller pieces I am left with on the jig.

Another feature of some saws is an adjustable clamp to hold down the work. This can be helpful to people who don't have strong hands. It is also useful when working on small pieces of wood. Although the force of the cut is downwards the blade can sometimes grab the work and the clamp will prevent this. Incidentally, should the blade snatch the work from your fingers, do not attempt to grab it back, which may be your first impulse, just switch off the power.

When cutting, as with all saws, let the saw do the work. This is particularly true with a fretsaw. Because the blade is so thin any force will bend it to one side resulting in inaccurate cutting. All you need to do is guide the work with gentle and downward pressure, one hand keeping the wood flat whilst the other steers it. If the blade is pushed to one side, relax and, just keeping enough weight on the wood with the fingertips to stop the saw grabbing the work, allow it

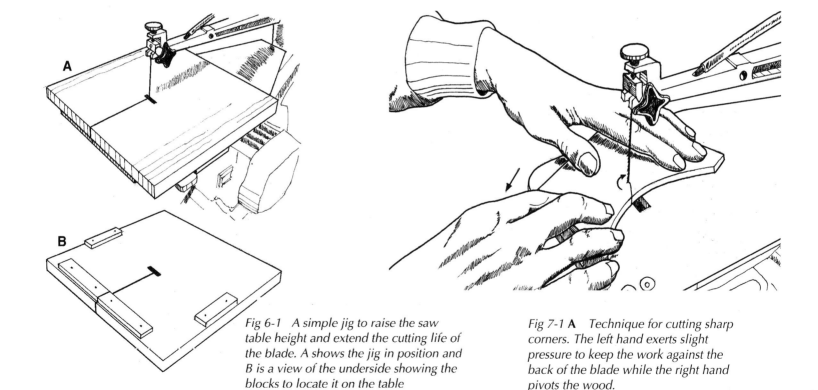

Fig 6-1   A simple jig to raise the saw table height and extend the cutting life of the blade. A shows the jig in position and B is a view of the underside showing the blocks to locate it on the table

Fig 7-1 **A**   Technique for cutting sharp corners. The left hand exerts slight pressure to keep the work against the back of the blade while the right hand pivots the wood.

to move back into true. With small pieces of wood the blade will move the work and correct itself, with larger ones you may provide a little assistance.

To turn the wood to cut a sharp corner exert gentle pressure towards you to keep the back of the blade against the wood. This prevents the saw cutting in to the piece until you have rotated it to the correct position. When cutting curves I find it helps to pivot the wood gently using the edge away from the cut, to give greater control.

One thing to note when cutting with a fretsaw is that the blade has a bias of a few degrees. The work has to be fed in at an angle which is slightly greater or lesser than a right angle in order to cut one.

For most purposes I use a number four wood blade. This is designed to cut wood up to 10 mm. thick but in practice it will cope with material up to 18 mm. if you cut slowly. Experiment, but cut with the finest blade you can get away with as, the finer the blade, the smoother the cut.

The small bandsaw

The final type of power saw that can be of use in making wood reliefs is the small bandsaw. Among its advantages are a good depth of cut, fine finish and squareness. Also, as the blade is a continuous rotating loop, all of it is used and it has a far longer cutting life than blades for either of the other saws.

It is not as manoeuvrable in cutting the work as a fretsaw because such fine blades cannot be used. It has the same limitations of depth of throat and it is impossible to use for making pierced work as the blade is a fixed loop.

Similar methods are used when handling the work on a bandsaw as for a fretsaw.

Choice of saws

In conclusion, if I were to choose one saw to do the work it would have to be the fretsaw. The best combination would be fretsaw and jigsaw, although a jigsaw bandsaw combination would be an acceptable though limited substitute.

With regard to hand saws I would suggest they are only useful in addition to a power saw. For example, if the only power saw available is a jigsaw, what can be achieved is considerably enhanced by the addition of a hand fretsaw. The majority of the cutting can be done with the jigsaw and any fine or intricate details added using the fretsaw. However to produce all the work by hand would require unlimited time and patience.

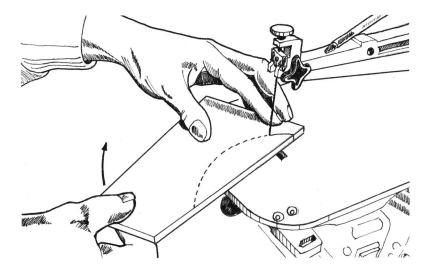

Fig 7-1 **B** *Technique for cutting curves. The left hand exerts gentle downward pressure while the right hand slowly pivots the wood as it feeds it into the saw.*

TOOLS FOR SHAPING

Power tools

Here my preference is just the opposite to the previous section. There are power tools to carve and sand wood but unless there is a very good reason I use hand tools. This is because most power tools that shape wood do so by grinding, thus generating vast amounts of dust. Some, in particular the router, are very noisy. The combination of noise and dust turns what should be a pleasant process into a stressful chore. However, they can have their applications so I will deal with them briefly.

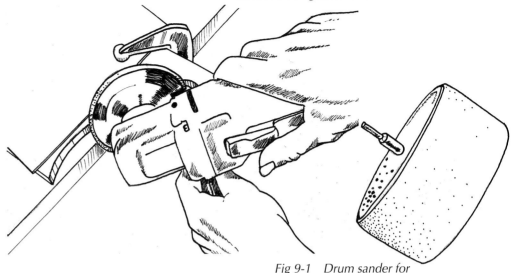

Fig 8-1   Illustration of sander and concave curve. The front edge of the disc sander is being used to contour the curve.

Fig 9-1   Drum sander for an electric drill.

ROUTERS

A router can be helpful for large scale work, in particular if a consistent moulded shape is required on the edges of the piece. I have used one to produce a bevel on a very flat relief that was both subtle and effective. However, it can only be used on relatively large pieces of wood that are firmly held. The cutter must be passed quite quickly and steadily over the wood otherwise it will burn it. This will necessitate so much labour hand sanding that it cancels out the advantage of using the router in the first place. This seems to be a particular problem with ply wood, perhaps because the glue holding the laminates together burns easily.

SANDERS

A small angle grinder with a disc sander attachment can remove large amounts of wood quickly with a coarse disc. This can make light, if dusty, work of shaping a built up part on a relief, particularly if it is made of laminated ply which is demanding to carve. Care needs to be taken on a concave curve not to let the edge of the sander dig in as it will quickly sand a groove that could ruin the wood.

Other sanders that may be useful are the disc and drum types which come as attachments for electric drills. The drum is particularly useful for giving a smooth finish over a large area or for finishing curves as, being without a hard edge, it cannot dig in like the disc.

Do be aware that power tools can be noisy and a machine such as a router may damage your ears if you use it without ear defenders. Both the router and the electric sanders create enough fine dust that it is also sensible to wear a filter over your mouth and nose. It is also essential that any work is firmly secured.

Hand tools

KNIVES

Hand tools are the mainstay for shaping the wood and in particular the craft knife. This is because the nature of the work generates small and often intricately shaped pieces that it is not feasible to fasten to a bench.

I generally use a Stanley knife for most whittling work, although a whole range of knives will work well. The main criteria, as with all cutting tools is that the blade should be sharp. It actually takes less effort and produces far better work if you take the time to sharpen a tool when the edge loses its keenness.

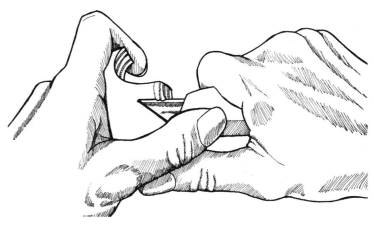

Fig 10-1   B: In this variation the fingers of the left hand and the thumb of the right clamp the work between them, while the fingers of the right hand hold the knife and the left thumb exerts pressure and control on the blade.

Whittling

As much shaping as possible should be done carving away from the body. The most power in a stroke is obtained by holding the knife in the fist and shaving downwards. More control is obtained by having the thumb up the back of the blade. At all times the other hand holding the work should be behind the knife hand.

When carving small pieces of wood the most controlled method is to curl the index finger of the knife hand over the front edge of the work. The thumb goes over the back, leaving the knife gripped in the other three fingers. The other hand, holding the work behind the blade, pushes the knife through the work with the

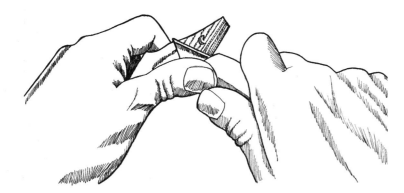

Fig 10-1   Carving away from the body. A: The fingers of the left hand grasp the work while the thumb controls the pressure on the blade of the knife which is held in the right hand.

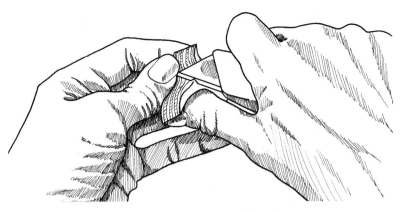

Fig 11-1 Carving towards the body. The left hand holds the work while the fingers of the right grasp the knife. The right thumb braces against the wood and pressure is applied to the blade by clenching the fist.

thumb. There are many slight variations on this particular carving grip, which is one of the most useful in relief carving work. The core principle however is that one hand holds the knife while the other pushes it, to achieve great control in cutting.

It is impossible to do all the whittling cutting away from yourself as the grain of the wood will not allow it. The action to use, when carving towards the body, is to hold the knife in your fist, blade towards you. Hook your thumb on the wood and pull the knife through the work towards it. If you are lucky the shape of the work will keep a piece of it between the blade and yourself. If not the stop for the blade is the ball of your thumb and extreme caution is needed.

With all whittling work do not be over-ambitious with the amount of wood removed at one stroke. Small shavings are best, exploring the vagaries of the grain. Too heavy a cut and the blade may well jam or split the wood in just the wrong direction.

Carving with the knife point

Most carving is done with the edge of the blade, but it is sometimes necessary to use the point. This is usually where some detail is to be added in the centre of a piece of wood and it is too fiddly to cut it first.

Don't cut too deeply or the knife will jam and you may snap the point off the blade. Just make a scoring cut and repeat it as many times as required. Make any cross cuts first so that they will act as stop cuts for ones with the grain, preventing the wood splitting further than required.

The cuts are made with the blade angled in to the work at about 45 degrees to make it easy to remove unwanted wood. When working in ply, once the cuts are through a layer of laminate the waste wood can be split out at the glue joint if it is a small area.

CHISELS AND GOUGES

When using chisels the work must be fixed to a bench in some way. Large pieces can simply be clamped down or grasped in the plastic stops of a Workmate.

Smaller pieces of wood can be held using a screw from underneath with a simple jig that is clasped in a vice (See inset illustration).

Fig 12-1

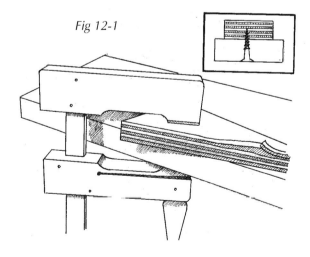

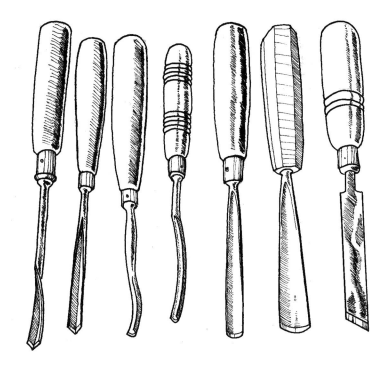

Fig 13-1   A selection of carving chisels. They are, from left to right, a front bent parting tool, a parting tool, a front bent veiner, a curved veiner, two gouges and a skew chisel.

A small range of chisels will cover most requirements in relief carving. The most useful is a shallow gouge with a cutting edge of about 20 mm. in width. This will take care of the general shaping work. Along with this a narrow gouge or veiner is needed for removing wood where there are tight bends in the cut shape. Another good chisel to have is a parting tool for making grooves, perhaps to add detail to an area where you don't want to make a saw cut.

Although those three chisels are probably the minimum you could get away with, there are many others which could prove useful. With a greater choice more wood can be accurately removed before having to resort to sandpaper.

Additional gouges are always useful with a good range of different curves, as are veiners. These are similar to gouges but with a deep, narrow, curved cutting edge. A selection of flat chisels and one with a skew end would complete the set.

Some carving tools come with the shanks bent either at the front or along their length. This is to enable them to be used in restricted spaces such as the inside of a bowl. They are fine for relief work, their only disadvantage being that they require more effort to use.

Incidentally when buying chisels and gouges, if you can find good quality second-hand ones they will be as good and often very much better than the new ones available today. This is because they were made by specialist tool makers who tempered the tool steel to the perfect pitch for the job. A lot of modern tools are designed for the DIY market and are made of unnecessarily hard steel that is brittle and once blunted, more difficult to sharpen.

Sharpening
Chisels and gouges used for carving are sharpened differently from ordinary carpenters' chisels in that the edge is honed from both sides.

To sharpen a gouge with an outer bevel (the most commonly used type) the bevel is honed on an oil or water stone. The gouge is pushed down the stone as if you are sharpening an ordinary chisel. However, as you push, the hand is rotated at the wrist so that the length of the curved edge of the gouge comes into contact with

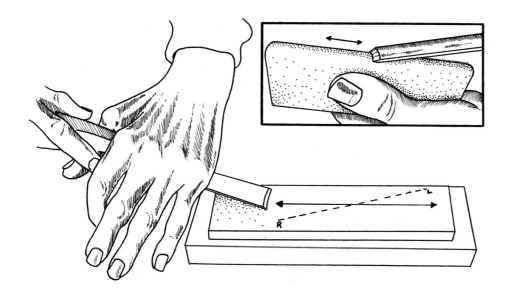

Fig 14-1 *Method of sharpening a gouge. As the tool is pushed down the stone the bevel is rolled from right to left. The motion is reversed as it is drawn back. It is important to move using the body, not just the arms, in order to keep the angle of the tool to the stone constant. The insert shows the inside edge of the gouge being honed on a slipstone.*

the stone at each stroke. As you pull back up the stone the motion is reversed. This must be done evenly in order to keep the profile of the blade square. The inside of the cutting edge is then sharpened with a slipstone.

The parting tool is sharpened on the oilstone just like an ordinary chisel except that care must be taken to hone the two sides equally in order to keep the profile square. The inside is sharpened with a slipstone. After it has been sharpened there may be a small protrusion at the point of the 'V'. This can be removed by honing on the oilstone.

Fig 15-1 *A: shows a gouge that has been sharpened too heavily in the centre causing it to dish. B: shows a gouge that has been sharpened too heavily on the edges rounding it. Neither of these will cut well though A is worst. C: shows a correctly sharpened gouge. D: shows an unevenly sharpened parting tool. It is important that each edge is ground down evenly. E: shows the spike left on a parting tool after the two sides have been sharpened. This should be honed off with a stone to produce F.*

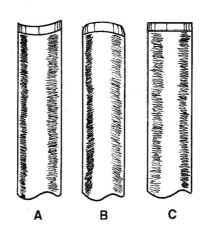

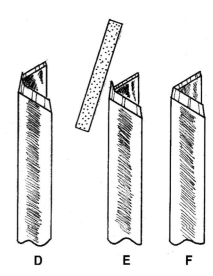

A   B   C   D   E   F

CARVER'S MALLET

The other ingredient to go with the carving tools is the carver's mallet. Unlike the normal mallet it is round and to my mind, infinitely preferable. In fact after using a carver's mallet for a while I could no longer use an ordinary one properly. Because it is round it has only one face and is therefore always correctly inclined for hitting the chisel.

I always make my own mallets and they are a simple enough exercise for anyone with a lathe. The best wood is lignum vitae but it is difficult to get hold of. I generally use fruit wood such as apple and pick a well sea-soned bit with small knots and wild grain as this inhibits splitting. However if you cannot get fruit wood many other timbers will do such as beech, elm or most hardwoods.

Turn the mallet in one piece so that there is no problem with the head flying off. The finished weight of one for use in relief carving should be about one pound.

Large quantities of wood are not removed from the work so a lighter mallet is less tiring to use and easier to control.

Methods of working

When using chisels with or without a mallet, as with whittling, do not try to remove too much material at once. Go gently and explore what is happening with the grain. Use soft firm taps with the mallet rather than hefty blows.

Using just a chisel to cut, one hand on the handle provides the push and direction while the other on the blade provides restraint and guidance. By twisting the wrist of the pushing hand when using a gouge, a rocking movement can be imparted to the tool, easing it through a difficult cut.

Whilst using a chisel never ever hold the work with one hand while you shave off a bit with the other, even if it's just a very tiny bit. Chisel and gouge blades make nasty cuts in flesh.

RASPS AND SCRAPERS

Other tools useful for shaping the wood are rasps and scrapers. Their purpose is to help smooth the surface, reducing the amount of sanding required. Rasps are the woodworkers' equivalent of metal workers' files and they come in much the same shapes and sizes. If not too much wood needs to be removed a coarse rasp will make short work of it leaving a finish that is quick and easy to sand. Surforms and Skarsten

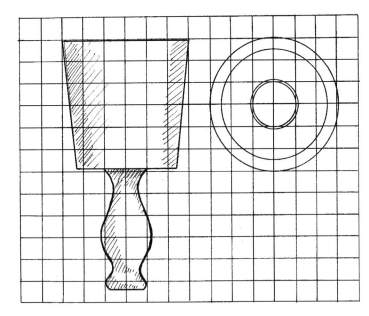

Fig 16-1   A scale drawing of a basic carver's mallet. Each division represents 2 cm.

Fig 17-1 A: *removing wood from the work with a shallow gouge and a carver's mallet. Note how the work is grasped with the plastic grips of a Workmate.*

Fig 17-1 B: *removing wood from the work with a shallow gouge. The right hand provides the force while the left steadies and guides the blade.*

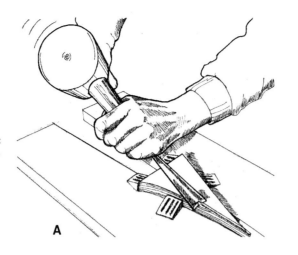
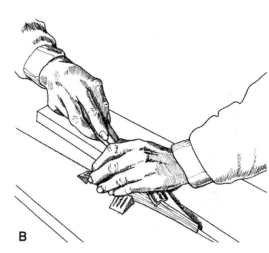

A

B

scrapers are good as they have replaceable blades and the Skarsten has a comfortable handle making it easier to use than a traditional scraper. Surforms come in a range of designs like files and planes and are used in the same fashion. A scraper is used by pulling it down the work towards the body keeping the blade at right angles to the wood.

Small planes, such as a block plane, also have their applications although they only work on a flat or convex surface of reasonable length. I suspect a set of thumb planes such as instrument makers have would be a joy to use but I have not yet had the opportunity to find out.

SANDPAPER

Finally the edges are finished with sandpaper. I use aluminium oxide paper; although it is more expensive than traditional sandpaper, it lasts far longer.

Where there are lots of tool marks or the wood has to be shaped entirely by sanding, because it is too intricately shaped to get a tool in, start with a 40 grit paper. On smoother parts use 80 grit and then finally finish with 120.

Fig 18-1 *Illustration of rasps and scraper. The top tool is a half round rasp. Below on the left is one of a range of Surform shapers and on the right a Skarsten scraper.*

2

MATERIALS

Plywood

The material I make most use of is birch ply as it has several advantages for painted relief work. It is a good quality plywood with close and evenly spaced layers that are generally sound. When the layers are carved through, they stand out like contour lines on a map. This is a

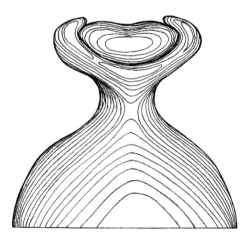

useful attribute that adds to the three dimensional feel of the work. The wood is almost white so it can be painted on with transparent glazes of colour without muddying them. Also the grain is energetic and varied and is often accentuated by the paint finish, helping to give life and energy to a picture.

There are many other types of plywood. The exterior and marine ones are generally too dark in colour to take paint well and should be used accordingly. Plywood also comes in a wide range of veneers and there is scope here for making pictures juxtaposing different wood colours and grains.

Fig 1-2 Shows the contour lines of a piece of carved ply. Each line in the illustration marks a glue joint in the plywood's laminations.

The main drawback about all plywood is the difficulty of working it from the carver's point of view. This is due to the laminate construction, with the grain in each succeeding layer being at right angles to the previous one. What tends to happen is that the cutting tool moving smoothly and easily through the grain of one layer hits the next one below and tears it. There are optimum angles to carve at to minimise this, but in practice when carving the edges of irregular shaped pieces of wood, tearing is unavoidable in places. The only way to overcome this problem is to carve the work leaving a tolerance where the wood tears and then sand it down to achieve a good finish.

When carving along the grain of plywood with a knife make sure you

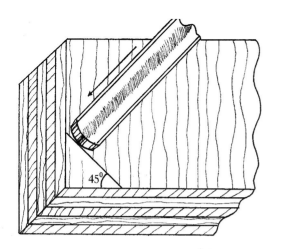

Fig 2-2   Shows the optimum angle for cutting plywood when cutting through two or more layers. Because plywood laminates have opposing grain the cut is angled at 45° to the grain's direction. The succeeding layer is at 90° to the one above and the chisel or knife blade also passes through it diagonally cutting the wood rather than tearing it.

avoid splitting it by always going in a direction that makes the knife cut slightly across it. The laminates of birch ply in particular are so thin that a split can run down the wood very easily.

You may also find when carving with the grain on the top laminate that as the knife cuts through it, it digs in to the layer below. If the grain is at just the wrong angle, the blade of the knife is pinched and it is almost impossible to cut. This is overcome by keeping the knife at a very shallow angle to remove as much of the top layer as possible

without penetrating the one below. Then at a steep angle the direction of the cut is reversed to bring the second layer flush to the first. These actions can be repeated until the required amount of wood is removed.

Wood

Carving with solid woods avoids the problem of opposing grain structure. Since there is not a great deal of modelling involved in relief work, it is not necessary to be quite so choosy as one would be about wood for carving in the round. In general any sound wood that is knot free and close grained may be used. Having said this, it will give you greater flexibility and ease of working if you use woods that lend themselves to carving. I list some woods and their general properties below.

Ash: Strong grain, light in colour, it takes paint glazes and stains well.

Basswood: A light, soft wood which is perhaps the most popular American wood for carving. Also known as American linden or whitewood in USA.

Beech: Very even grain, its golden brown colour will mar light colours and stains.

Butternut: An excellent N. American carving wood. Medium brown in colour and easy to work.

Elm: Dark in colour with wild grain, poor for stains and glazes, also difficult to carve as the grain keeps changing direction.

Fruit woods such as apple, pear, damson, plum, cherry: Grain varies, pear wood can have really beautiful figuring, all have brown colour, all carve well, although the wood is soft it is close grained and does not tear.

Lime: Light in colour and marking so it takes paint glazes and stains well, carves very well.

Maple: Light in colour with strong grain so it takes paint glazes and stain well, very hard, slow to cut and carve.

Oak: Medium to dark brown in colour with strong grain, particularly beautiful when quarter sawn so that the medullary rays in the wood's structure are revealed, but poor for glaze and stain, carves well.

Pine: Generally light in colour, sometimes with strong grain, takes glazes and stains well, mostly too soft to carve well, but because of this softness is easy to sand down. Choose close grain pieces that are knot free.

Walnut: Dark in colour with sometimes beautiful grain, poor for glaze and stain, carves well.

Yew: Varies greatly in colour, the outside can be light while the heartwood can be anything from dark brown to purple, with a strong wild grain, very hard, carves well.

Tropical Hardwoods: Generally dark in colour, some such as mahogany and teak carve well. Be wary of them as some are poisonous, splinters go septic and dust from them may be harmful. When buying new wood you should ensure that it comes from sustainable sources where replanting takes place.

Many other woods are suitable. I would encourage you to experiment. If a piece of wood fits the work and it won't carve, sand it; if it's too dark give it a colour glaze with white in it or try bleach to lighten it. Also the darker the stain or glaze to be used, the less the existing colour of the wood effects it.

Other wood-type products

Apart from wood I also use other wood-type products. I use hardboard and medium density fibreboard mainly as backgrounds to stick on all the other pieces. Hardboard is also useful for blocking up work that only needs to be raised slightly.

I use MDF in the picture if I am using a paint effect or collage that completely covers it. As a material it is soft to cut and sand and takes paint well, as it is dead flat. A sanded edge will need a second wipe with fine grit paper after a coat of paint. If you are cutting MDF with power tools or sanding it, use protection as it generates very fine dust.

Fillers

Sometimes it may be necessary to use filler. Even the best birch ply can have a knot hole in a laminate. I always use a two pack resin filler. Although it is expensive it bonds strongly to the wood and is stable. It can be carved and sanded and takes paint well. The filler is very unlikely to be a perfect colour match and it clouds the grain so any surplus should be scrupulously removed by sanding it well back. This is particularly important if the finish to be used on it is transparent.

Material sources

Because the wood used in reliefs can be in quite small pieces a lot of material can be acquired for little or nothing. Good sources are the scrap piles of joinery firms, shop fitting companies and skips. I call in at a friend's joinery company and rummage around in his offcuts pile and he is amazed at the wood that I find useful.

The fact that such small pieces of wood are usable may cause problems as it can be difficult to decide what should be burnt or thrown away. My workshop generally has boxes of offcuts which accumulate over the summer months. Were it not for the winter and the need for heat I would eventually have no room to work at all. It always seems to happen that when I finally get around to burning something, lo and behold, the next project creates a perfect use for it.

Other good sources of materials are old rejected pieces of furniture. I have gleaned some lovely strips of oak from old wardrobes. Sometimes they even have mouldings or details on that may be exploited in a picture. Do not disregard material with printed patterns on it, it may be used to build up other work as a base, or if the pattern is interesting perhaps as a background in a still life.

Even a formica top or a piece of lino may turn out to be useful. I particularly like material that is pretending to be something else, such as hardboard that has a printed surface to mimic woven raffia and plastic that looks like cloth or leather.

3

PAINTS AND FINISHES

ACRYLIC PAINT

The bulk of my work is finished with paint and generally acrylics are the chosen medium. I use them because they can be diluted with water and are fast drying. They seem as flexible in use as oil colours without the need for volatile thinners and cleaners and can be applied thickly to produce dense colour or thinly as translucent glazes and washes.

A wash is a thin mixture of paint that is translucent and the colour of the background shows through it. On birch ply it allows the grain to show through and sometimes enhances it.

A glaze is similar except that the term is usually applied to a colour that is painted on top of another that is already dry. For example a translucent glaze of blue is painted over a layer of yellow to produce green.

The advantage acrylics have over ordinary water colour is that once dry they are waterproof and will not re-dissolve when another colour is painted over the top of them.

Colour palette

A basic colour range would be ultramarine blue, vermilion hue and cadmium yellow medium. These together with titanium white and lamp black or Payne's grey will allow you to make a broad range of colours and tints. I have suggested Payne's grey as a substitute for black as when applied densely it is very dark. However when applied thinly, as it is a blue grey, it makes much more convincing shadow tones than black.

Useful additional colours to extend the palette would be crimson, Hooker's green, olive green and some of the earth colours such as yellow ochre, raw sienna and burnt umber.

Unless you are an experienced colourist keep your selection of pigments limited until you become familiar with them. In this way you will build up a solid understanding of their properties. Mix colours carefully and don't use too many at once or you will end up with mud. In general try to mix no more than two pigments at once. You can always modify the colour later with a glaze.

I suggest you buy artists' colours. They may be dearer but they will contain more and better pigment and will last you longer. Make sure you select colours that are permanent. All colours have a permanency rating and some colours are fugitive. This means that they break down and fade in sunlight and are therefore not suitable for work intended to last.

Brushes

I use pure sable for fine points and a sable ox mix for the larger flat brushes. However, good quality synthetic blends made specifically for acrylics are an acceptable economic substitute.

The minimum number of brushes you could get away with would probably be three. A sable point, size number three, a 9 mm. sable ox flat and a 20 mm. sable ox or ox flat. The point is obviously for fine detail, the small flat for general work and the large flat for colour washes and varnishing. Buy the best brushes you can afford and make sure by wetting them that they come to a good shape with no forking. Get them with long hairs, they will last you longer, hold more paint and are more flexible to use.

As you progress and become familiar with the material you will add other brushes to these but they are a good basic start.

Mixing colours

You will find the paint is reluctant to dissolve in water and must be mixed with persistence. If you are making a translucent glaze it is better to add the water a bit at a time until the pigment is well dissolved in order to

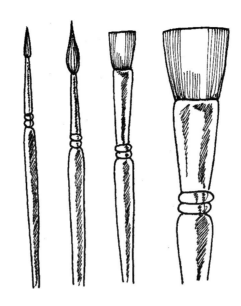

Fig 1-3   Illustration of brushes showing from left to right a no. 1 sable point, a no. 3 sable point, a 9 mm. sable ox flat and a 20 mm. sable ox flat.

disperse it evenly. Test it first before you apply it to the work to make sure the tone is correct. This is particularly important with a first coat as the wood is absorbent.

Beware also of little clots of undissolved pigment in your brush, you may need to wipe them out on a rag. If you do get a streak of pigment on the work fill your brush with clean water, work it over the paint and it should diffuse in to the surrounding area. Glazes generally dry lighter and paler than they appear when wet.

Colour mixing by laying one glaze

over another, say red over yellow to make orange, can often be more effective than simply mixing them in the palette. The light from the one colour glows through the other giving a feeling of depth.

When painting very thin washes or glazes it is important to be aware that too much dilution with water will thin the binding material in the paint to a point where it will no longer fix the pigment to the work. If the dry painted surface is rubbed with a finger and particles of colour come off, this point has been reached. In this case an acrylic painting medium should be used in conjunction with the paint and water.

For a palette I use a selection of plastic lids as they are readily available and free.

Applying colours

I generally paint in the shadow areas first using Payne's grey and then the local colour of the object over the top. This is done before gluing so that the carved edges can be done easily and neatly.

If the wood needs detail painted on it such as brick or stone work it is a good idea to seal it with a glaze of colour to inhibit its absorbency so that the delicate work does not blot or blur. I often use a thin glaze of raw sienna for this purpose.

Should you wish to diffuse the edge of an area of colour or blend it into another one, wet the surface where you want this to happen when you apply the pigment and it will blot in to it. Similarly, if you want to apply a colour wash to a large area, if you wet the surface first it will help you to spread the paint evenly. The edge or a whole area of paint can be softened by blotting it with a rag.

If you feel a colour is wrong and cannot be corrected by overpainting you can sand it off. When it is dry use 120 grit paper sanding in the direction of the grain.

I add the highlights last using titanium white and adjust the shadow areas. This is done when everything is stuck down. White over a colour can seem quite opaque when wet but may almost disappear when dry. This is useful when painting clouds as the centre parts can be built up with several coats, leaving the thinner areas around the edge to diffuse in to the background.

Finally, the relief is signed, dated and varnished. I use an acrylic varnish, because it is quick drying, touch dry in ten minutes, and water soluble when wet.

At the end of a painting session brushes should be thoroughly cleaned using washing up liquid. This is worked well in to the hairs undiluted to remove any traces of pigment and then flushed out with cold or tepid water. The brushes are gently stroked into their correct shapes and left to dry.

OTHER FINISHES

Oil colours

Oil colours can be used in much the same way as the methods described for acrylics. However the drying times are longer and there is the problem of volatile and potentially hazardous fumes from the thinners and cleaners.

Wood stains

The same short-comings are true of wood stains and they have the added limitation of a small range of colours. They may well have their application in a piece which is largely reliant on the different colours and textures of natural woods. However, unless you are familiar with their use I would tend to experiment with the earth colours of acrylics as a more user friendly substitute.

Natural wood finishes

The simplest durable method is probably several coats of varnish. If you like the sheen and smell of polish then one coat of matt varnish will seal and protect the wood from marks and leave a surface with enough bite to take a coat of wax. This can then be buffed up to give it lustre. I use a sheepskin pad on an electric drill.

If you want to feed the wood, brush on a coat of boiled linseed oil and leave this as the finish or when it has thoroughly soaked in apply a coat of wax polish over the top. Alternatively apply one or more coats of teak oil.

Specialist finishes

This is far too broad a topic for me to cover thoroughly here. However there are one or two techniques that I make fairly frequent use of which are described below.

Eggshell

This is my somewhat coarse adaptation of an ancient Chinese technique which they used to produce exquisite lacquer boxes and objects. I use it to create an interesting textured surface that is a pleasant contrast to the wood.

Collect the eggshells, clean them by washing them in water and allow them to dry. Break them into pieces about 15 mm. across and using P.V.A. glue stick them on to a board. I generally use MDF as it is flat and they adhere well. The pieces need to be pushed flat by cracking them. This can be done with the thumbnail or using a smooth instrument such as the handle of a tea spoon. As they are pressed down the glue will squirt out of the sides. This is blotted up with a damp cloth.

Do not be too concerned about fitting the pieces together perfectly. Any big holes can be broken up with small bits of shell later and the other gaps will form a web of lines like a large version of the cracks in the shells. Only apply the eggshell to the parts of the board that will be seen as it is a time consuming process.

When you have covered the required area with shells allow the glue to dry. Then paint over it with your first colour. This will probably be a dark colour such as Payne's grey. Use a 9 mm. flat brush and

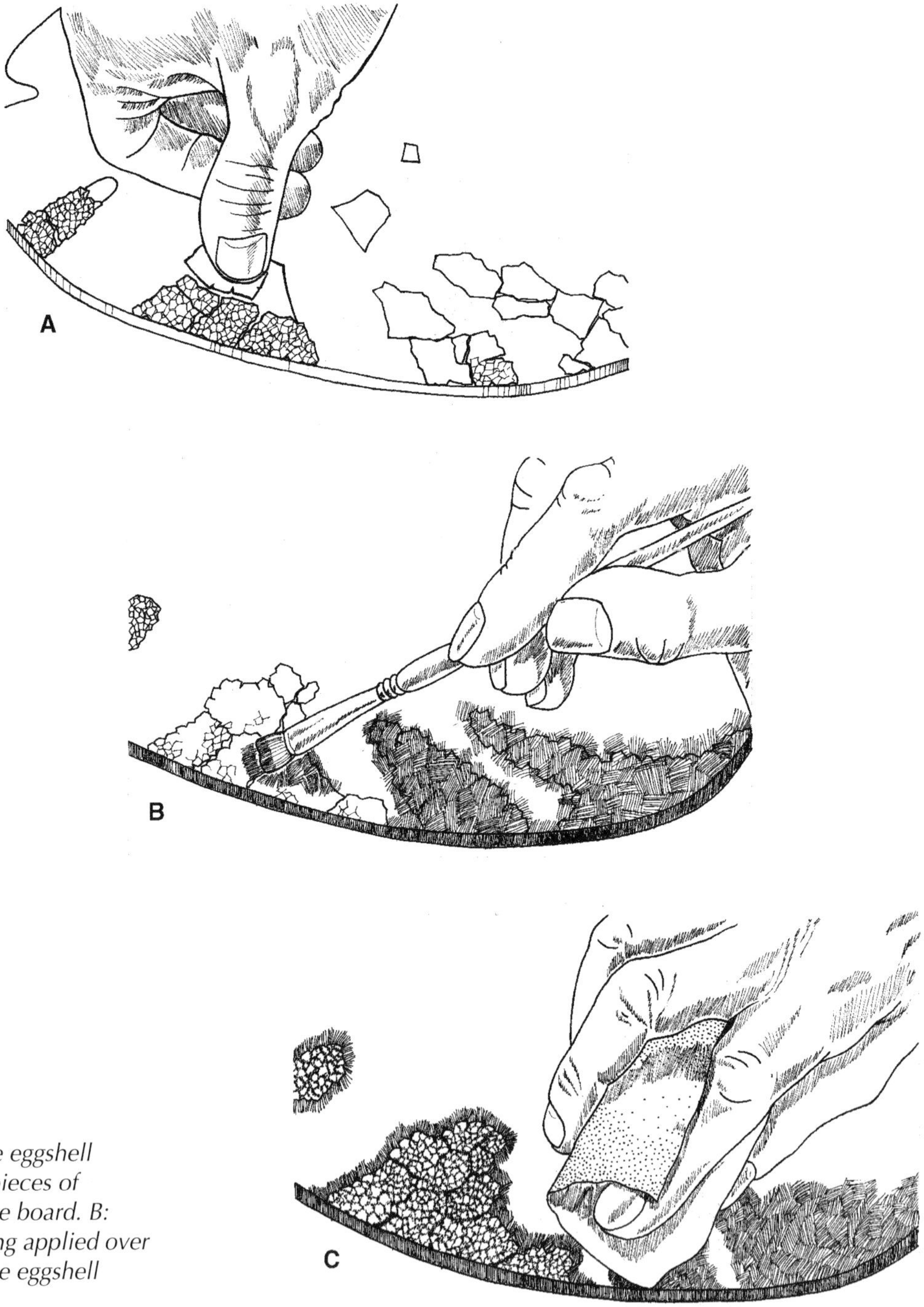

Fig 2-3   Illustration of the eggshell technique. A: shows the pieces of eggshell being glued to the board. B: shows the first colour being applied over the eggshells. C: shows the eggshell being lightly sanded.

make sure you work the paint well in to the cracks.

When the paint is dry sand over the surface with 120 grit paper. Then add your next colour. You can repeat this process and use several colours if you wish. If you want to create some highlights give it a final very gentle sanding.

Eggshell can be applied to curved surfaces provided the curves are gentle and not much rounder than an egg. Concave surfaces are more difficult as they go against the natural curve of the shell, but they are still possible using small pieces from the flatter part of the egg.

Rag rolling

This is actually a decorator's technique for painting walls but I find it useful for backgrounds of still lifes or for interiors.

I use emulsion paint for the process and apply the paint with a small foam roller designed for use with gloss. This gives a very nice finish on MDF producing a texture not unlike good quality cartridge paper.

Apply the background colour using the emulsion straight from the tin. If I am painting a small area I just dip the end of the roller in the paint, then spread it on the board. This saves

paint and avoids dirtying a roller tray.

When it is dry, paint a glaze of thinned emulsion over the top. This is immediately rolled over with damp disposable kitchen cloths — I use 'J-Cloths' which are gently crumpled in to a wad and pushed over the surface with the flat of the hand so that they roll. The damp surface of the cloth picks up the wet paint in an interesting pattern allowing the background colour to come through in varying intensity. Vary the direction of the cloth as it is rolled to

avoid a linear design.

The amount by which the emulsion is thinned when used as a glaze coat is a matter for experiment. It can be diluted by as much as ten parts' water to one part paint. The thinner the glaze the more translucent it is and the more the background colour shows through.

When working with paint this thin, it is best to have the board horizontal, and if you are applying the paint with a roller, do so very gently or paint will spray everywhere.

Fig 3-3   Illustration of rag rolling technique

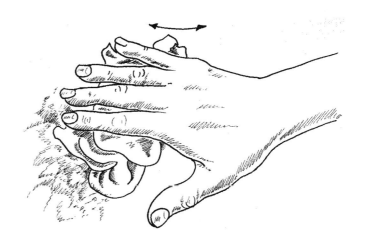

Dragging, stippling, sponging and spattering

These are all very similar to the rag rolling technique described above. Only the way the glaze is treated varies.

In dragging, stroke over the glaze with a large damp brush. This pulls the glaze into lines not unlike the grain in wood. Always run the brush the entire length of the work before lifting it.

With stippling, tap firmly with a stencil brush or special stippling brush on to the glaze. This pushes it in to little flecks.

A sponge is used dabbing down on the glaze to remove it. Alternatively the glaze is applied with the sponge. The best texture is achieved with a real sponge as opposed to a synthetic one. A J-Cloth can also be used in this fashion and it will produce a texture similar to stippling. Another alternative is a plastic bag. This is crumpled into a ball and patted on to

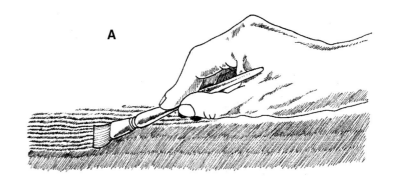

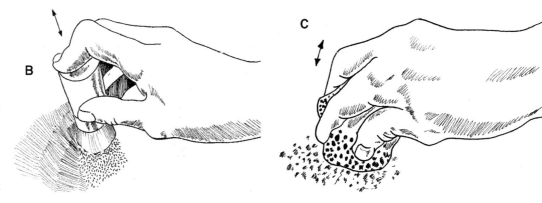

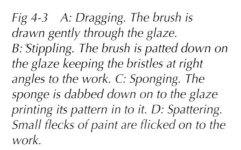

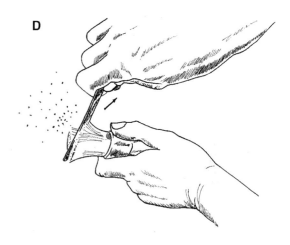

Fig 4-3   A: Dragging. The brush is drawn gently through the glaze.
B: Stippling. The brush is patted down on the glaze keeping the bristles at right angles to the work. C: Sponging. The sponge is dabbed down on to the glaze printing its pattern in to it. D: Spattering. Small flecks of paint are flicked on to the work.

the glaze. Occasionally wipe the bag off and re-wad it. This technique will produce a texture similar to rag rolling but more defined.

For spattering, a stencil brush is dipped in the glaze and a table knife or other flat instrument is dragged back through the top of the brush. As the brush hairs spring back small blobs of paint are flicked on to the work. This is a particularly effective way of impersonating stone when several different glazes are used. If the colours are still wet they will bleed in to each other.

Always try a trial flick before spattering the actual work. If there is too much glaze on the brush or the mixture is too thin it will produce great streaks and blots rather than small spots.

Gold leaf and Dutch metal

I will touch on this subject briefly and in the most basic of fashions. I use Dutch metal in pictures from time to time to simulate the brass of a trumpet or the gold of an Icon. Dutch metal is the poor man's gold leaf and is applied in the same way. Unlike the real thing however, it will slowly tarnish unless protected from the air by a coat of varnish.

I use transfer leaf as opposed to loose leaf. Because it is attached to paper it is much easier to handle.

The wood to be treated should be smooth and sealed either with varnish or paint, yellow or red being good colours. It is worth giving the work several coats of paint and sanding down with fine grit paper between each one, producing a flat well-sealed surface which is ideal for the leaf. It cannot be stressed too strongly that the smoother the surface the better the leaf will look and the easier it is to apply.

A layer of japan gold size is applied thinly and evenly over the surface with a brush. The size is allowed to dry until it is tacky. This point is tricky to judge because if it is too wet or dry then the gold will not stick properly. I test it by touching it gently with a knuckle. If there is a slight adhesion to the skin then the size is ready. The process should be carried out in a dust and draft free environment.

The transfer gold is cut to about the right size and shape and gently placed on the work. It is pushed on with a soft dry brush and the paper removed. When the area to be treated has been covered with leaf it is brushed over thoroughly to smooth it down and remove any overlapping material. This is done gently but persistently and the brush will

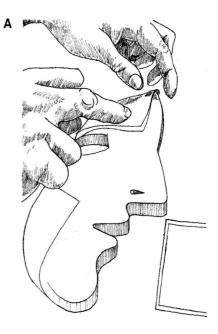

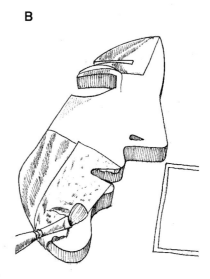

Fig 5-3   Illustration of gold leaf application A: shows the transfer leaf being applied to the work. B: shows the leaf being smoothed on to the work with a soft brush.

gradually flake the surplus leaf off. Any places where the leaf has not adhered can be touched up with a spot of size and a scrap of leaf.

Silver leaf is available and the method can also be used to attach silver, gold or aluminium foil. Foil can also be stuck on work using an adhesive such as 'Copydex'.

Collage

I use collage in many of my pictures, particularly ones containing buildings. Putting collage behind the windows is an easy and interesting way to create pictures within pictures and add depth to the design. Combining odd objects or using images that are on a completely different scale to the rest of the picture can give a surreal dimension to the work. A huge head, for example, looming from a window catches the viewer's eye, intrigues their mind and lures them in to the picture.

I collect material by cutting out images that interest me as I come across them and filing them. I also search through piles of magazines with a specific theme in mind. These may include reproductions of paintings, posters and prints, interesting and brightly coloured patterns and famous people or characters, real or fictional. The main criteria is that the images are small and well defined.

As paper stretches when it is wet, care needs to be taken when gluing it. Absorbent paper such as newsprint should be wetted and left for a minute or two before being glued and stuck down. It will then shrink as it dries and stretch tightly. All material should be thoroughly coated with glue. As it is stuck down it should be rubbed firmly with a damp cloth to get any wrinkles out. It is the same process as wallpapering but on a much smaller scale. If the paper is not stretched and glued well and the collage is varnished it may well bubble up and dry that way. P.V.A. or heavy duty wallpaper paste are good adhesives.

Fig 6-3   Two examples of collage use. A mock front page of a newspaper and some sheet music form the background for this fret cut trumpet.

Pictures cut from an astronomy magazine with the addition of some flying saucers make the background for this picture of a fairground ride.

4

DESIGN

Methods using drawings and photographs

When I am creating an original design I make a series of drawings of the chosen subject. I move around to change my viewpoint and if a particular part of the composition looks good from one place I will draw it. I don't aim to be precise in the sketches but try to get the feel of the subject. At the same time I may well take photographs and make written notes on colour, especially if the subject is a landscape.

I spread out all the material I have and examine it. Then I make drawings from my sketches, notes and photographs combining bits from the different sources together. Initially I do this with the basic shapes, distorting them where necessary to make them fit together. I may cut up the photographs and juxtapose the bits. Eventually when I have some pleasing combinations I re-draw them as one picture.

I may just produce a simple line drawing indicating the saw cuts and refer to my other drawings and photographs for any other information. However if I want to experiment with various textures and patterns I will make a working drawing including them.

Fig 1-4   A working drawing (overpage)

A COLOUR ROUGH

If the subject does not already have a clearly defined colour scheme or I am not sure how I want to treat it I will make some colour roughs. These could take the form of quick sketches in felt tip pen or I may use acrylics to get a more precise idea. With the acrylics I would use a heavy water colour paper such as 'Bockingford' as it has a nice texture allowing for dry brush work and enough weight to take the wet paint without buckling.

A good way to approach a colour rough is to follow the procedure for painting outlined in Chapter 3. Put the shadow areas in first and add any local colour you are sure of as light washes. This will give you a feel for the colour balance of the picture.

If you prefer to paint on a smooth and lighter weight paper such as cartridge you should stretch the paper first. This is done by thoroughly soaking the paper and laying it out on a board. A braced drawing board is preferable so that it will not warp. The paper is stuck to the board with brown gummed paper tape and left to dry. The paper will shrink taut on the board and be held there by the tape.

*Fig 1-4   Working drawing
for a lilies project*

SCALING UP

At this point the drawing size is usually quite small, probably A4 or less. I now put a grid on the sketch using a pencil or make a tracing and put a grid on that. The scale of grid I choose depends on the complexity of the design, but generally it will be about 1 cm. squares. I then scale it up and make a full size drawing on tracing paper. This may seem like a lot of drawings to make for one picture, but each time I re-draw it I have the opportunity of refining the composition and making it work better. It is best to spend the time at this stage getting it right as once you start cutting it is far more difficult to change things.

Fig 2-4   Example of a scale drawing

TOOLS FOR SCALING UP

The minimum tools you require are a ruler, set square and pencils. It makes the whole process much quicker and easier if you have a drawing aid with some form of parallel motion for the small scale grid. I use a plastic A3 drawing board with a sliding ruler on it for the initial drawings. For larger drawings and transferring work to the wood it is useful to have a metre rule or a long straight edge and a tape measure.

TRANSFER TO THE WOOD

The full scale drawing is now transferred to the wood. Do this by going over the lines on the reverse side of the tracing paper with a pencil, HB or softer. Then placing the drawing on the wood, correct way round, go over the lines with a ball point pen. Then re-draw the lines on the wood with a fine felt tip pen refining them yet again and also defining the picture clearly for cutting on the saw. Just leaving the transferred pencil mark gives a rather faint outline that may be smudged with handling.

Other methods

Perhaps you are not confident in your ability to draw from life. I would urge you to have a go. Draw something or somebody you really like or try a simple still life.

Just because a drawing is not realistic in the classically accepted sense does not mean it is valueless. Naive painters and childrens' art have things to tell us about the way we think and view the world.

After all, perspective does not really exist. The railway lines don't meet on the horizon. Things do not shrink as they get further away from you. Children know this and it shows in their pictures. They also know that a car has four wheels so they put them on it when they are drawing even if, from the viewpoint they are depicting it, only two can be seen. As they are drawing they are putting down not just what they see but what they instinctively know. We all do this to some extent, but the process is more marked in children and naive painters. Most adults have been educated in to a classical way of viewing the world and artists like Picasso have gone to a great deal of trouble to break free from this and re-capture their childhood spontaneity.

Perspective is just a technique to impersonate the way we see and to give an illusion of distance.

The fixed viewpoint is also a classical pictorial convention. In reality everything changes from moment to moment no matter how still we try to be. Anybody who tries to paint a landscape quickly realises this. We are not motionless and neither is anything else. A lot of the art of the twentieth century has been concerned with coming to terms with these truths.

Some simple drawing exercises

Pick a simple object, a bottle for example. Place your pen or pencil in an appropriate place on your paper and draw the object's outline. Do this without looking at the paper. Instead stare at the object and as you draw imagine your pen travelling round its edge until you are back where you started, then look down. Fill in any detail you want to add in the same way. Ignore any inaccuracy in your first line and place your pen as near as possible to the correct place.

At first your drawings may be quite chaotic, but if you persevere, after a few attempts you will be surprised at their accuracy. The important thing is to maintain your concentration. As your drawings improve try more complex subjects and combinations of objects.

Set up a simple still life and light it in a contrasting way to generate strong shadows. Draw what you see only by shading in the shadow areas. Shadow is what gives the eye information about shape. Again as your drawings improve try more complex subjects including people if you can get someone to sit for you.

Pick a selection of objects for their variety of textures and patterns and draw them concentrating on these aspects. Progress on to landscapes and analyse them in the same way.

These exercises should, with practise, improve your drawing

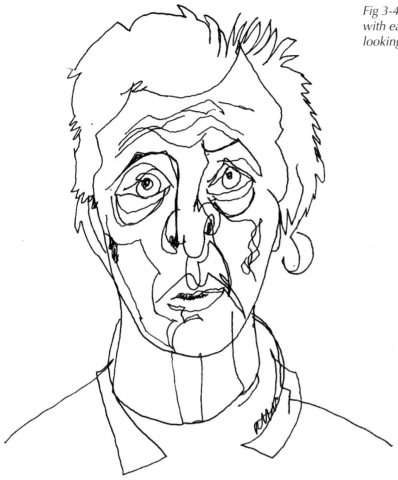

Fig 3-4 An example of a drawing made with each line being drawn while looking at the subject and not the paper.

Using a projector

If you have access to a slide projector, you can project your negative or transparency on to a sheet of paper or even directly on to the wood itself and draw round the image. The difficulty in this lies in deciding what to put in and what to leave out. Only practice will help you here, but a good idea is to put in the major outlines of things first and then add only the detail necessary to make the drawn object recognisable. Remember that what you are drawing is a cutting line and that if you intend to paint the finished work a lot of information will be conveyed by colour and shadow. The main function of the cutting line is to distinguish objects or distinct parts of objects and allow you to model them to suggest their shape.

A light box

Should you find yourself producing a lot of designs from slides it is worthwhile making a light box. I did this as an aid to producing the illustrations for this book.

The light box is a frame supporting

abilities, sharpen your perception of the way you see the world and your understanding of what makes things look the way they do.

Using photographs

If you want perspective in your work and lack the technical ability you can make designs from photographs. This can be done by tracing directly from colour prints and then scaling the drawing up as described earlier. You can also use this method to combine several pictures.

a sheet of glass over a mirror set at an angle of 45 degrees. The projector is placed with its lens close to the mirror and the light is reflected on to the glass above. When you lay tracing paper on the glass it acts like a back projection screen. This allows you to draw your image in a comfortable position without the problem of your own shadow coming between you and the picture.

The framework is constructed in 50 x 25 mm (2" x 1") soft wood with 6 mm. MDF or plywood providing the walls of the box and giving it rigidity. 6 mm. thick glass is used for the screen and it is positioned within strips of beading. The glass is big enough to allow an A3 drawing to be made. In my light box I use a shaving mirror mounted in an adjustable frame so that I can alter its angle.

Distortion

If you are using a projector you can exaggerate and distort perspective in your composition by tilting the board you are projecting on to, in order to make your picture more striking. If you have made a light box you can do this by changing the angle of the mirror.

You can achieve the same thing using a grid. For example a still life you are making has an open book on a table. The blocks of wood representing the pages are cut in perspective, to make the book appear to be coming forward out of the picture. You want to paint a picture on one of the pages in the right proportions. Draw the shape of the page, dividing each side in to equal sections and join the divisions to form a grid. Draw a straightforward grid over the picture you want to use and then copy the image on to the page altering it to fit the distorted grid.

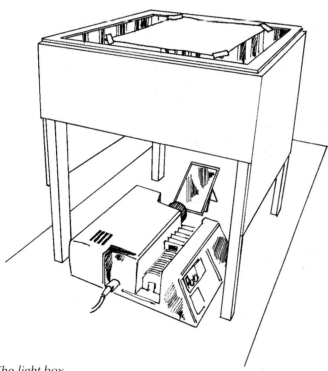

Fig 4-4   The light box.

Fig 5-4 A: A straightforward drawing

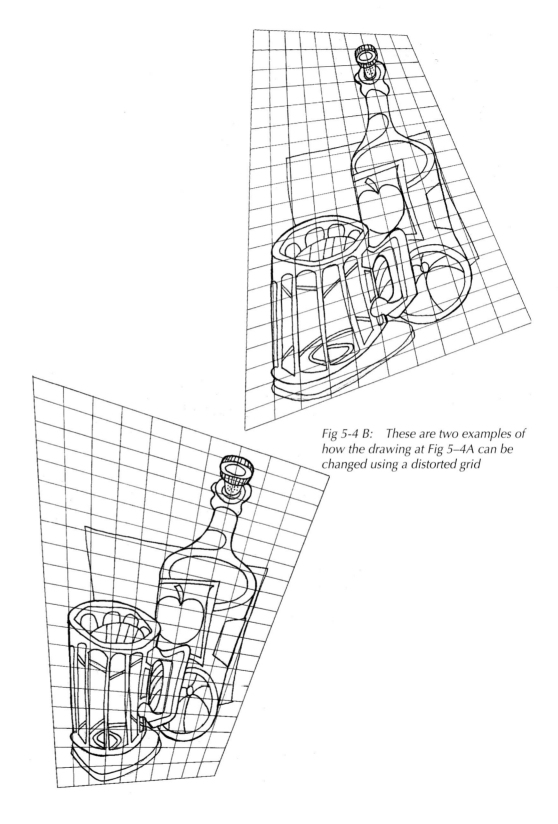

Fig 5-4 B: These are two examples of how the drawing at Fig 5–4A can be changed using a distorted grid

Silhouettes

Another method of making designs, particularly for still lifes, is to draw round silhouettes. If you set up a strong light source on the objects to be drawn you can then draw the outline of the shadows. This will give you the proportions of the subjects accurately making it easier to fill in the details. This can work very well for flowers which are often recognisable just from their outline. Glasses and bottles are also particularly good as you can get interior detail from them as well.

Composition

When you are creating a design of your own try to be aware of what your eye does when looking at it. Ideally your vision should be led into the picture and then allowed to tour round it without any obvious means of escape (Fig 7-4).

If you find you drift in to the picture then out of it again, identify the place where you leave and put something there to block the exit. See the illustration at 8-4 for an example of how a line, which would otherwise send the viewer's vision straight across the picture, is interrupted.

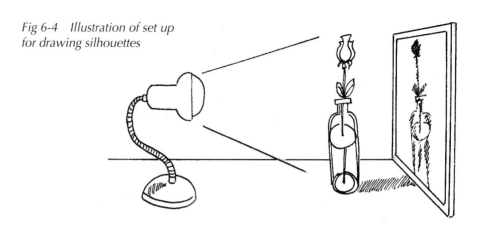

Fig 6-4   Illustration of set up for drawing silhouettes

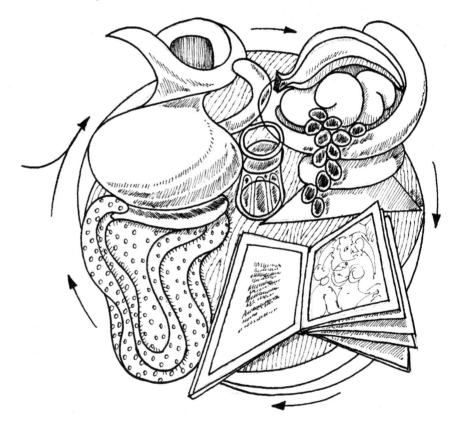

Fig 7-4   Illustration of good composition and how the eye is led around it.

You should also be conscious of balance in the design. A good way of checking this is to look at it in reverse. Hold the drawing up to a mirror or if it is a tracing turn it over. If it still looks comfortable to the eye the picture is balanced. If however it seems to lean over or appear too heavy in places some adjustment must be made. Do be aware however that the composition may not work quite so well. We are accustomed to scan things from left to right because of the way we read and your picture may well reflect this.

In landscapes, place something in the foreground on a much greater scale, such as foliage or a window frame, to add depth to a picture. You can experiment with this by cutting different foreground objects out of paper or card and trying them in various positions in conjunction with your picture (See Fig 9-4).

The Belgian surrealist painter René Magritte used window frames and the view through them to great effect in many of his pictures.

It is also important to let some objects overlap others and the relief process can help to emphasise this.

Lastly, don't be afraid to change or modify your ideas as the work progresses. I often add to, or subtract things from pictures. Something

made for one picture that isn't quite right may be just the thing for another one. Have the confidence to experiment.

Fig 8-4   This composition is dominated by horizontal lines and in particular the line of the kerb. If this was not broken by the strong vertical of the stop sign and the wall to the right of it, the eye would run straight across the picture.

Fig 9-4   This picture uses a foreground still life and a window frame to give added depth and space to the landscape. See projects 4 and 5 for other examples of the same device.

Texture and pattern

As has been noted in a drawing exercise, texture and pattern are important elements in a composition. Different textures give variety and depth to a picture. As well as using some of the decorative techniques described in Chapter 3, try using the brush in different ways. Paint can be dabbed on, it can be dragged on as a dryish mix to pick up the texture of the wood. This can be very effective when an opaque colour is painted over a translucent one as it emphasises the depth in the clear glaze. Brush strokes can be cross hatched, varied in shape and size and follow or contradict the contours of the wood.

Simple repetitive patterns, such as stripes and spots work well. Flowers made of four or five dabs with a brush for petals and a blob of different colour in the centre can bring a picture alive. Pattern can be introduced in many places. It is all around us in the man-made things of the world.

Collage and mixed media material can also be used to generate texture and pattern. Experiment with the addition of different materials such as plastic, leather, metal and stone. Old sandpaper glued down and painted with Payne's grey simulates a tarmac road very well.

COLOUR

Colour can be exploited to enhance the composition and mood of a picture.

Primary and secondary colours

The colours of the spectrum are derived from white light. White splits into three primary colours. These are red, yellow and blue and cannot be made from any other colours. They can however be mixed and any two of them produce a secondary colour. Blue plus yellow makes green, blue plus red makes purple and red plus yellow makes orange.

Complementary colours

Complementary colours are opposites. They are made up of one primary colour and the secondary colour made by mixing the two remaining primaries. Red is paired with green, blue next to orange and yellow next to purple. When they are used in conjunction with each other, such as red and green stripes, they are visually exciting and appear to move. The purer the colours the more effective this is. In the case of the red green combination the red should be a pure spectrum red and the green mixed from a blue and yellow, neither of which should contain any hint of red pigment.

Colour temperature

All colours have 'temperature', some are warm and others cool. In general colours at the red/yellow end of the spectrum are warm and those at the blue end are cool. Of course there are exceptions, it is possible to have a cool yellow or red and a warm blue.

Cool colours are visually recessive and warm ones assertive. If you had two identically sized rooms and painted one in cool blue and the other in a hot red, the red room would appear much smaller than the blue because the hot colour would seem to bring the walls closer to the eye.

This property of colour can be exploited in pictures to enhance the feeling of space. Objects that are to appear near to the viewer are painted in warm tints while distant things are painted in cool ones.

Colour temperature can also affect mood or the feeling of a picture. Cool tones are restful or sad while warm ones are jolly or aggressive. These are somewhat crude generalisations, the subtleties of complete colour theory being beyond the scope of this book. However, if you observe the use of colour with these thoughts in mind it will help you to utilise some of its properties and may open your eyes to others.

Copying

It is perfectly acceptable to copy existing pictures that you like, always provided, of course, that you keep within the laws of copyright and that you're not trying to pass off your work as someone else's.

As Picasso said: "What does it mean for a painter to paint in the manner of So-and-So or to actually imitate someone else? What's wrong with that? On the contrary it's a good idea. You should constantly try to paint like someone else. But the thing is you can't! You would like to. You try. But it turns out to be a botch . . .

. . . and it's at the very moment you make a botch of it that you're yourself."

The copy will almost always turn out to be a different picture. This is particularly so if you make your copy, as a tracing for example and then put aside your original source. By the time you have scaled the drawing up, transferred it to the wood, the combination of your own unconscious modifications and errors coupled with the changes wrought by expressing the picture in a different medium will have created a new work.

The other aspect of copying someone's work is that, by observing it closely, you will gain a greater understanding of their techniques. This can only be helpful to your own development.

By attempting to copy a Picasso picture and turn it into a relief, one of the things I gained was a great appreciation of how he could convey enormous amounts of information about a subject with a few deceptively simple brush strokes.

I would suggest that if you do decide to make copies, or interpret other people's work, to start with you choose bold, well defined pictures. These should be ones that lend themselves to the relief process. Picasso's work is a good example as are the graphic works of Toulouse-Lautrec and the paintings of Gustave Klimt.

Another artist whose work is relevant is Jean Arp. He made wooden fret cut reliefs of organic but abstract compositions. They are painted in flat colours, deceptively simple and well worth looking at.

The art of the distant past is also a rich source of ideas. Classical Greek painted pottery with its bold designs or the Assyrian reliefs mentioned in the introduction spring to mind.

5

THE WORKING PROCESS

Assembly

A design is chosen or created, scaled up and transferred to the wood.

The design is cut out and reassembled to form the picture. It is worth noting that if the design is a complex one involving lots of pieces it is a good idea to reassemble it as you go. Alternatively, divide the picture up in to sections and as you cut each section up place the bits in a bag. You may end up with half a dozen bags full of wood but it will considerably simplify the jigsaw puzzle you have made for yourself.

Building up the relief

At this point you may want to build up some parts of the relief if you have not already created different levels by using various thicknesses of wood. There are alternative ways to

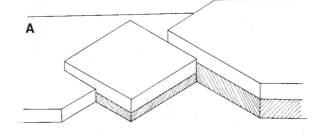

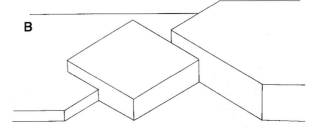

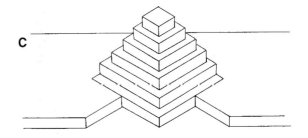

Fig 1-5   The three methods of relief construction. A: The work is cut from one sheet and packed from behind using material of varying thickness. B: The relief is constructed of wood of different thicknesses cut to fit next to each other. C: The work is cut from one sheet and additional material is glued to the surface to create varying thickness.

do this, either by packing out from behind or by building up the front.

If you are packing the work out from behind, select pieces of scrap of the correct thickness and draw out the shape on them using the cut pieces as a template. The packing material will only need to be cut to the exact size if it is protruding above the surrounding pieces, otherwise it is simpler to cut it out slightly smaller.

If you are building up from the front, again use the cut piece as a template but cut the piece out smaller. How much smaller will depend on how far back you plan to carve the wood. A good rule of thumb however is to reduce it by less than the thickness of the material. If you are using 6 mm. ply for example, reduce the piece to go above it by no more than 4 mm. all round.

Glue the built up pieces together using P.V.A. and clamp them or place them on a flat surface and put weights on top. I have a collection of chunks of steel and heavy pebbles that I use for this purpose.

Shaping, painting and gluing

All the separate pieces are now carved and sanded. Next they are painted around their edges and faces with shadow and background colour. How far you carry the painting process before you glue the bits down will depend on the design of the particular relief you are making, but all the edges must be painted.

Any collage or mixed media you are using may be added at this stage.

As the pieces dry they are glued and clamped or weighted down.

The painting process is completed. Final adjustments are made to shadows and the highlights are added. When all is dry the finished work is varnished. It is often a good idea to hang the picture for a while before varnishing as you may see things you would like to alter after it is in situ.

If necessary, changes can be made after varnishing. If the paint will not bite on the varnish the surface can be given a key by a light sanding with 120 grit paper. I have to confess to going back to and changing pictures as long as two years after I have made them. I sometimes even remove whole sections with the deft application of a chisel and replace them with something different.

Frames

Some reliefs may need the additional structure or support of a frame to show them to their best advantage or just to keep them flat.

There may be problems using traditional framing methods due to the nature of the piece. For example you may have a great variety of depth in the composition. The best

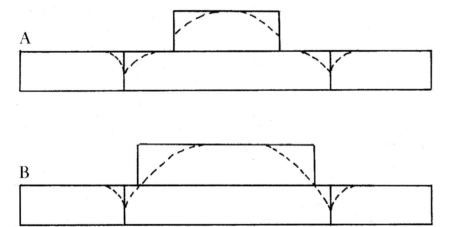

Fig 2-5   Sections showing the importance of keeping the additions on a built-up relief large enough. The dotted line indicates where the carving would come. A: The added block is too small and a step is left. B: This is correct and only a minimum amount of wood need be removed to create a smooth curve.

solution in this case could be to frame it with a mitred box.

If there is plenty of depth of wood around the edges and it is a good fit, glue alone should be sufficient to hold everything together.

If you do not possess a set of frame clamps a simple way to apply pressure while the glue sets is to use a loop of cord and a length of dowel. The work is set up on a bench with one side close to the edge and glue applied to all the necessary places. The cord is arranged loosely round the box or frame and knotted to form a loop. The dowel is slipped through the cord and twisted so that it winds the cord up. As it is wound up the cord will pull tighter and tighter round the box.

When it is exerting firm pressure all around the work the piece is simply slid further on to the bench to prevent the dowel turning and the cord unwinding.

The corners of the frame should be protected with corrugated card or scraps to protect them from damage when the cord is wound tight.

This method can also be used to make a hidden frame or to reinforce an irregular shaped piece. Care needs to be taken that the frame remains square if the work is not fitted inside when you are gluing it.

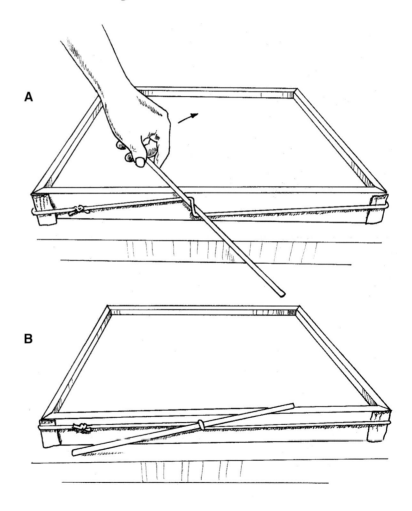

Fig 3-5   This shows a simple method of clamping a mitred box or frame whilst gluing. Note the scraps of cardboard on the corners to protect them. A: shows how the dowel is slipped through the cord. B: shows the work slid back on the bench to hold the dowel and prevent the cord unwinding.

PROJECT 1

DESERT ISLAND

This is a good project to start with as the piece is built up in layers and the paint is applied as areas of flat colour. This provides an easy introduction to the tools and materials used in relief work. It can be made even simpler by omitting the eggshell and using flat colour instead. Another interesting alternative is to replace the painted plywood sun with a smooth light coloured pebble. The finished work can be decorative or serve a functional use as a bookend.

Materials

Birch ply: 18 mm. **x** 250 **x** 180,
6 mm. **x** 320 **x** 240.
MDF: 18 mm. **x** 480 **x** 360,
12 mm. **x** 440 **x** 320,
6 mm. **x** 320 **x** 240.

Wood glue, eggshells (optional). Paints comprising Payne's grey, titanium white, cadmium yellow, ultramarine blue, olive green, Hooker's green, raw sienna, vermilion red and acrylic varnish.

Method

Scaling up and cutting out

This relief is constructed using woods of different thickness planted one on top of another as shown in the drawings.

Scale up the drawing from the book on to tracing paper and then transfer it to the wood as described in Chapter 4. To make it the same size as the original and to fit the specified materials each square on the drawing represents 4 cm.

Cut the sky and the palm tree leaves from the 18 mm. MDF.

Cut the eggshell background from the 6 mm. MDF. This piece is still needed even if you do not wish to eggshell it.

Cut the dark green leaf shapes and the spiky orange plant from the 12 mm. MDF.

Cut the palm tree trunk, the rocks and the desert island sand from the 18 mm. birch ply.

Cut the sea and the sun from the 6 mm. birch ply.

Scale drawing of project

Scale drawing of project with assembly details

CARVING AND SANDING

The sea, sand and rocks have a simple bevel carved on their edges. This is whittled with a knife and sanded, the radius of the bevel being adjusted to the thickness of the wood. Be sure to carve only the exposed edges and in the case of the sand taper the bevel off towards the back. The sun also has a bevel carved on both inner and outer pieces.

The place where the sun is located in the sky needs to be hollowed out if you are using a pebble instead of plywood. This is best done with a mallet and a gouge. Place the pebble in position on the sky and draw round it with a sharp pencil. Make another line about 4 mm. in from the first one and start your carving from there. Make your cuts from the outside to the centre. Keep trying the pebble in the hollow until you get a snug fit.

The trunk of the palm tree is also carved and this is slightly more complex as notch cuts need to be made for the dead leaf shape and the coconut. To cut the leaf make a 90 degree cut in to the wood at the bottom of the shape as a stop cut and then shave up the trunk to it. Keep deepening the notch cut as you

model the trunk. The nut shape is made in the same way but the notch is carved away on both sides to create the roundness of the nut and to give some shape to the top of the leaves.

All the carving is sanded down with 80 and then 120 grit paper.

If the background is to be eggshell this is done using the method described in Chapter 3. The dark green leaf shape that goes above it should be placed in position and drawn around so that only the exposed board is treated. Glue the eggshells past the drawn line to ensure good coverage.

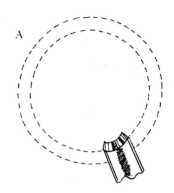

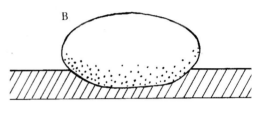

Method for insetting a pebble for the sun. A: The outside dotted line is the one drawn round the pebble. The inside line is the actual cutting one. B: Shows the pebble inset in section

Carving in to the notch on the palm tree trunk. The arrows indicate where the stop cuts come.

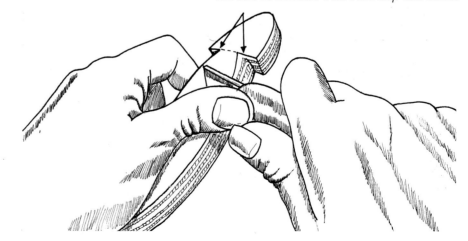

PAINTING AND ASSEMBLY

All the painting except for the varnish is done before assembly. The paint for the MDF should be applied quite thickly. It may need more than one coat depending on the colour and absorbency of the material. The edges will almost certainly require two coats and may need a light sanding in between. You may wish to mark where the next layer comes in order to paint only the exposed area. If you do, make sure the work is marked only lightly in pencil, or that the line will be covered by the piece above, as it may show through the paint.

With mixed colours try and ensure that enough colour is made to cover in one go as it is very difficult to mix more to an exact match.

The sky is painted with a mixture of ultramarine blue and titanium white at a ratio of one part blue to four parts white. Paint the edge also.

The eggshell background is given a coat of Payne's grey. This is lightly sanded when dry and followed with a glaze of ultramarine blue. Both colours go over the edge. If eggshell is not used then the board is painted blue and then a glaze of the grey over the top.

The edge of the dark green leaf shape is painted orange, a mixture of one part vermilion to three parts cadmium yellow. This same colour is also used for the face of the spiky plant. The face of the leaf shape is painted with Hooker's green.

The palm leaf face is painted with a mixture of olive green and cadmium yellow at a ratio of three yellow to one green. This is also used for the edge of the spiky plant. The edge of the palm leaf is painted olive green.

The plywood pieces are painted with a thinner paint finish to allow the wooden laminates to show through.

The sea is painted ultramarine blue and the sand cadmium yellow. The outer circle of the sun is vermilion red and the inner titanium white.

The trunk of the palm tree is raw sienna and the rocks are painted with a thin glaze of Payne's grey. They have some white highlights added when the grey is dry.

The pieces are now glued together. This is done in several stages.

The orange spiky plant is glued to the dark green leaf and the leaf to the eggshell background.

At the same time the sand is glued to the sea.

The palm tree leaf is glued to the trunk and the rock to the front. These are then glued to the orange plant. They should be weighted down or cramped until the glue goes off. Care must be taken that all the bottom edges are in line and square.

The sand and sea are then glued to the plants making sure the backs are flush.

Then the sky is glued on the back and the sun glued on the sky. If you are making the pebble version it is best fixed using a blob of silicone.

Finally when the glue has gone off the whole piece is varnished. Do not be tempted to varnish the work before it is glued together as the varnish will greatly reduce the adhesive power of the glue.

A colour illustration of the project appears on p 92.

PROJECT 2

STILL LIFE: FRUIT AND WINE ON A TRAY

This project is a relatively simple one to make, but if it is executed life size or larger it will make an effective piece, perhaps for the dining room wall.

Materials

Birch ply: 18 mm. **x** 400 x 250
12 mm. **x** 250 x 150
6 mm. **x** 250 x 150

MDF: 6 mm. **x** 250 x 200

Ash edging strip:
4 mm. **x** 20 x 2050

Plywood or board with veneer or patterned surface 600 x 420 mm.
Wood glue.
Eggshells.

Paints comprising Payne's grey, titanium white, cadmium yellow. ultramarine blue, Hooker's Green, crimson, raw sienna.
Collage materials for the bottle.

Method

Scaling up and cutting out

This relief is constructed using woods of different thickness and also by blocking up, so some pieces need to be cut twice.

Scale up the drawing from the book on to tracing paper and then transfer it to the wood as described in Chapter 4. To make this piece the same size as the original and to fit the materials specified each square on the drawing represents 2.5 cm.

Cut the bottle, fruit and the wine glass goblet and stem from the 18 mm. birch ply. The goblet of the glass and the left-hand peach also have backs cut from the 6 mm. ply to raise them. In the case of the glass the 6 mm. ply has a circle cut from the middle and removed so that the part of the relief representing the inside of the glass drops down in it.

Cut the base of the wine glass and the back of the right-hand peach

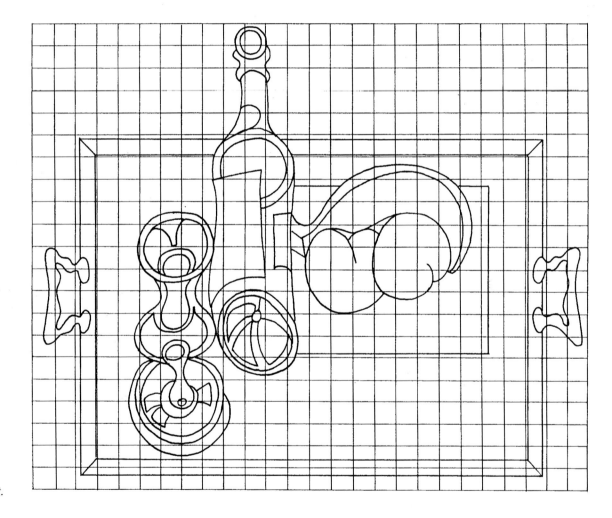

Scale drawing of project.

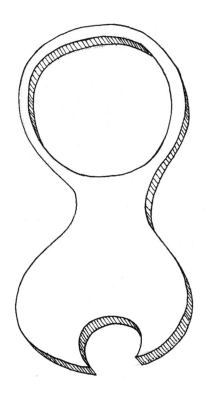

Blocking up piece for the wine glass. Note that a piece is removed at the top to inset the contents of the glass.

helpful where pieces fit together snugly, as in the case of the fruit, to cut them from the same piece of wood so that the saw cut forms the joint.

Where the fruit and glass are being blocked up by extra plywood and this wood can be seen, cut the top pieces first and then draw round them on to the blocking up wood with a sharp pencil or a ball point pen. When you stick the two pieces together shave off any little discrepancies in size with a knife or by sanding.

Cut the tray out of your chosen background material and cut out a piece of thin scrap in the shape of the bottle neck. This should have a generous flap at the bottom of it so it can be glued to the back of the tray.

from 12 mm. birch ply. Cut a board for the fruit from MDF and cover it in eggshells where they can be seen as described in Chapter 3. Cut the tray edge from the ash strip and make the handles from 6 mm. birch ply.

If you have one, I would suggest you use a mitre saw or block for the corners on the ash edging. It is also

Blocking up details. The part of the wine glass and the peach with the diagonal shading are blocked up with 6 mm. ply. The crosshatched peach is raised with 12 mm. The pieces forming the neck of the bottle, indicated with dots, go on to a backing of 4 mm. scrap. This is cut as shown on the left and the part below the neck glued to the back of the base board.

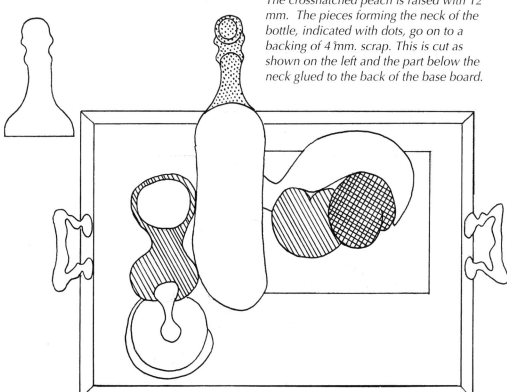

Project cut and part carved

CARVING, WHITTLING AND SANDING

I chose relatively thick wood to make this still life because the majority of objects in it are round. This being so it is a good opportunity to exploit the contour effect of the ply wood layers by cutting quite deeply into them.

For the banana and the two peaches use a shallow gouge and carver's mallet to remove most of the wood. The peaches should have their backing pieces glued on before they are carved. The ply is gripped in a vice or the plastic wedges of a Workmate to hold it. Tidy up the places that need it with a sharp knife and then sand the fruit to a smooth finish.

The rest of the pieces are really too small to grip and work on easily with a gouge so whittle them to shape with a knife and then sand them.

Incidentally you may notice that I have not shaped the two pieces of wood that form the labels on the bottle. This is because I want to emphasise their squareness in contrast to the roundness of the bottle.

Carving completed

ASSEMBLY AND PAINTING

The bits are now reassembled, but nothing should be glued at this point except for the ash edging strip on the front of the tray and the thin piece to support the bottle neck on the back.

Paint on the shadows using Payne's grey as shown in the illustration. I used an 8 mm. sable and ox hair brush for this to keep the strokes quite bold. The board covered in eggshell is also given a coat of the grey, working it in to the cracks well as it forms the background colour.

If you are using collage as I have done for the wine labels now is the time to apply it. The gold border which I have used was made to follow the cut curve at the bottom of the label by making a series of cuts

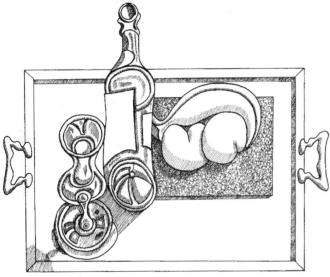

The shading on the illustration indicates where the shadows are painted

Grey painted

in it. If you don't cut completely through the paper it helps to keep it aligned when you stick it down. The more cuts you make the closer it will follow the curve. I kept the cuts down to a minimum because I think it gives the lines a jerky energy.

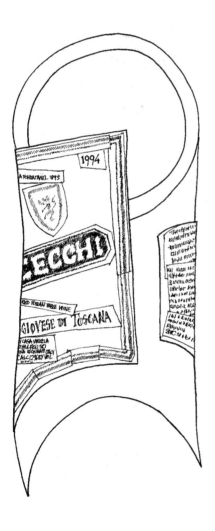

Detail of the collage on the label. Note the cuts to curve the paper strip forming the border.

Now apply the local colours on top of the shadows. Crimson is used for the wine. As this is a translucent red it should be applied fairly thickly in order to give strength to the colour.

Paint the bottle with Hooker's green, the green going over the crimson of the wine on some of the pieces.

Paint the banana with cadmium yellow

The peaches are painted an orange mixed from cadmium yellow and crimson at about six parts yellow to one part red. When this is dry, wet the peaches all over with water and brush crimson on next to the shadow areas. Because the surface is wet it softens the brush strokes allowing the colour to diffuse at the edges and appear to blend with the orange below.

Paint the glass with some strips of the green and red to reflect the bottle and the wine. The rest of it is painted with raw sienna to give a hint of the colour of the tray below.

The handles of the tray also get a touch of raw sienna as do the wine labels.

Sand the eggshell down using fine grit paper and give it a coat of ultramarine blue.

All the pieces can now be glued together.

When the glue is dry, any final shadow areas missing, such as the ones of the fruit on the eggshell, are added and any other colour adjustments made.

Now the highlights are added with titanium white. Paint a yellow-white mix on the fruit next to the white highlight to soften it.

Finally sign and date the picture and give it a coat of varnish.

A colour illustration of the project appears on p. 92

PROJECT 3

RECLINING WOMAN

First sketch

This is a more complex project entirely made from plywood. The roundness of the design exploits the contour lines of the wood's laminates.

The picture can be treated either as a free standing piece or mounted on a background and framed. A variety of colour schemes and paint methods are described to illustrate the basic properties and possibilities of acrylic paints.

Materials	Varnish, wood glue
	Paints comprising Payne's grey, titanium white, cadmium yellow,
Birch ply: 9 mm. x 600 x 600	
6 mm. x 600 x 800	vermilion red, ultramarine
4 mm. x 400 x 400	blue, Hooker's green, raw
12 mm. x 250 x 250	sienna, burnt umber.

Scale drawing of the project. The shaded areas indicate where the wood is removed to reveal the backing board. The dotted areas show where the wood is removed altogether in the free standing version. The pieces shown on the side are bits that are added on top rather than built up from behind. The eyes, eyebrows and nose are 4 mm. ply and the finger is 6 mm. ply.

Method

SCALING UP AND CUTTING OUT

Enlarge the drawing and transfer it to the 9 mm. birch ply. Transfer the outline to the 6 mm. ply. To scale it up to the same size as the original and to fit the materials specified, each square on the drawing represents 3 cm.

Cut the pieces out. You may find you need to make some cuts with the jig saw in order to make manageable sizes for the fret saw. Do as much as possible on the fret saw by running in the cuts from different directions.

On the face, the nostrils and the inside of the ear are removed with piercing cuts. The eyes, eyebrows and nose are cut from 4 mm. ply.

The little finger of the hand under the chin is cut from 6 mm. ply.

THE BLOCKING UP

Make all of the blocking up pieces by using the already cut out work as templates. Draw round them precisely with a sharp pencil or ball point pen and then cut the work on the fret saw with the cut running just on the inside of the mark.

The arm on the right (her left) is blocked up with 4 mm. ply except

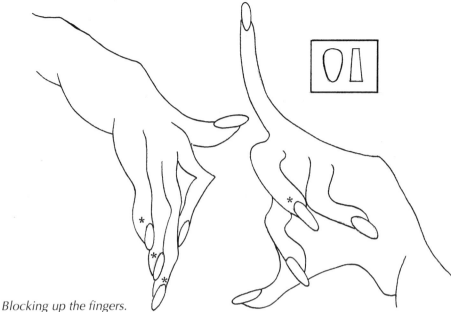

Blocking up the fingers.
The asterisks on the drawing indicate which fingers are blocked up. The drawings in the inset box show the wedge-shaped blocking up piece in plan and section. As the finger nails are cut and shaped separately the blocking up pieces should be made generously enough for the nails to be glued to them.

for the finger under the chin. The third finger is raised higher by gluing a piece of 4 mm. scrap between it and the 4 mm. board. The scrap should be shaved to a wedge shape. The work will need to be securely cramped while gluing to force the finger up. The finger below should not be glued on until it has been carved. The sleeve for this arm is packed out with 6 mm. ply

The other arm is also backed with 4 mm. ply and small scraps placed beneath the tips of the lower three fingers to force them proud. It is sensible to carve them first as it will

help to make them flexible.

The roll of sleeve nearest the arm is blocked up with 6 mm. ply and the one below with 4 mm.

The whole of the head and the hair on the left-hand side is backed with 6 mm. The fringe and the lips are raised a further 2 mm. with some scrap. If no wood is available a piece of card will work just as well in a situation like this where the edges will not be seen.

The breasts and the parts of the dress covering them are packed out with 6 mm. ply and the knee is backed with 12 mm.

Wood cut and carved

CARVING

All of the carving could be done with a knife. However if you have a shallow gouge it makes sense to use it where a comparatively large amount of wood is removed, such as along the jaw line.

Some of the carving is quite difficult because on the round pieces there are places where the opposing grain causes problems. This is overcome by removing the first layer with a shallow cut in one direction and the succeeding ones with a steeper cut in the other, as described in Chapter 2.

Where wood needs removing from the saw cuts between the fingers and the spiral cut in the hair, this is done with the tip of the knife blade. The left thumb provides the force behind the knife.

Care must be taken with the carving on the face. While quite a lot of wood is removed from the jaw line and the top of the head only a slight bevel should be put on the point of the chin and the nose. The lips must also be approached gently. I recommend offering them up to the rest of the face frequently while working on them, in order to make fine adjustments. The removal of very small amounts of wood can make great changes.

In my view the human face is the most rewarding but also the most challenging of subjects. Expression is conveyed by the most subtle variations in shape and line. It takes very little movement to change a smile to a scowl.

ASSEMBLY

If you wish to make this a free standing piece it gives the whole work a better finish if the backing board is cut, sanded and shaped to fit along the edges. This is achieved by gluing the pieces on in stages.

The whole picture is assembled in order to locate everything correctly. Then the two arms and the knee are glued on and held in place with cramps. The rest of the pieces are then removed so that they are not accidentally stuck.

When the glue is set more pieces are added that coincide with the edge. Any parts of these which touch bits already glued on should have their edges painted. This is particularly important where the pieces represent different things, dress next to hair for example. It may be difficult to get paint in the joint later, as the joints are quite deep and paint may go where it is not wanted.

Once all the pieces that come on the edge are stuck on, the edges of the backing piece can be rounded off with a knife and then sanded to a good fit.

If you wish to glue it on to an ordinary background it is best to follow the normal procedure of doing the majority of the painting before sticking the pieces down. She would look effective against a rag rolled background done in light colours.

The shading on the illustration indicates where the shadows are painted.

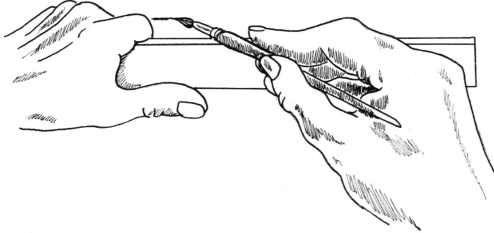

A simple method for painting straight lines with a brush. The fingers of the left hand curl around the ruler raising the front edge from the work. The ferrule of the brush is run along the ruler generating a straight line. (This is particularly useful for the green and red dress version).

This shows the technique for painting simple flowers using a round brush. As the paint is applied in one stroke, the larger the brush size the bigger the flower will be. A: The brush is pushed down vertically to make the round centre of the flower. B: The brush is pressed down on its side, with the point towards the flower's centre to create a petal. (This particularly applies to the red dress with yellow flowers)

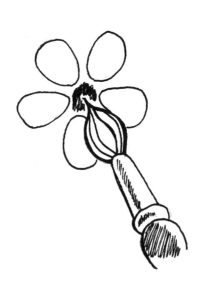

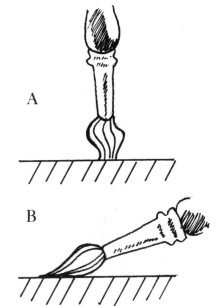

A

B

PAINTING

As can be seen from the colour plate on page 65 I have included colour roughs of four different ways of painting the woman.

GREEN AND YELLOW DRESS

This picture shows a relatively simple paint treatment for the figure.

The edges of all the pieces are painted with Payne's grey. The shadow areas of the skin are painted with a mixture of ultramarine blue and white. A simple flesh tone is made by using raw sienna with white, the highlighted areas being created by the addition of more white to the mixture.

The hair is painted by applying some simple brush strokes of vermilion and then adding a glaze of raw sienna.

The lips and fingernails are vermilion with white highlights. The eyebrows, lashes and pupils are done in Payne's grey as is the inside of the ear.

The dress is painted with a mixture of Hooker's green and white and this is also used for the iris of the eyes. The stripes on the dress are cadmium yellow with a line of burnt umber either side of them. They are applied to emphasise the shape of the body, giving the picture a soft curvaceous feeling.

GREEN AND RED DRESS

In this version as before, the edges are painted with Payne's grey.

For the skin small amounts of ultramarine blue, vermilion red and cadmium yellow are squeezed on to a palette together with a larger amount of white. The shadow areas are painted first, mixing some blue in to the white. Then red is added to more white and the remains of the blue mix and this is painted next to the blue while it is still wet, so that the colours blend together to a degree.

Apply the colours reasonably strongly and if you feel they are not blending together well enough, wash the brush out, wipe it with a rag and brush over the colour join. The clean and relatively dry brush will drag the colours together. If you want to soften the colour joins even more, you can do this by dabbing or gentle rubbing with a finger or a cloth.

Next add yellow to the white and lay it on next to the red, blending it in. Make another red mix for the cheek.

Provided you work reasonably quickly the paint will stay wet long enough for you to return to areas to adjust the colours as you go along. Use a brush size appropriate to the scale of the work.

This method works on the principle that white with a small amount of blue, red and yellow added to it makes a convincing flesh tone. More blue in the mixture makes the cool tones of shadow areas, more red gives the warm pink of cheeks and yellow the glow of light.

It takes a bit of practice to master the technique and if you have never painted in this way before I strongly recommend spending some time experimenting first. Try different consistencies of paint to see how they blend. It will repay the investment as the process has many applications and gives a more lively and interesting finish than the simple colour wash method.

The eyebrows, lashes and pupils are painted with Payne's grey. The iris of the eye is ultramarine with a white highlight. The hair is painted cadmium yellow with raw sienna brush strokes and white highlights.

The dress is painted with Hooker's green mixed with white and vermilion red in stripes. The aim is to mix the green to make it complementary to the red. The shadow areas have a glaze of Payne's grey.

In this version I have made no attempt to follow the implied contours of the body under the dress. I have applied the pattern as if to a series of flat surfaces. The contradiction imparts a visual tension. This together with the stronger areas of colour in the flesh makes for a harder, more angular feeling in the picture. This could be increased even further by substituting all the curves for a succession of straight lines and eliminating any warm tones in the colours.

BLUE DRESS WITH WHITE SPOTS

The same technique is used for the skin as in the previous version with the addition of raw sienna to the palette. This helps to create the warm and darker flesh tones.

The hair is painted with Payne's grey and burnt umber and then has white highlights added. The pupils are painted with Payne's grey, as are the lashes and eyebrows. The iris is burnt umber with a white highlight.

The dress is painted ultramarine blue with white spots on top. The shadows are a glaze of Payne's grey.

RED DRESS WITH YELLOW FLOWERS

The skin is painted using the same technique as described for the previous two versions, with the addition of burnt umber to the palette. This darkens the skin tones even further but still keeps them warm.

In this treatment the colours are not blended one into another so fully. This leaves more clearly defined brush strokes, which although they are not so naturalistic, give energy to the picture.

The hair is painted with Payne's grey over a wash of ultramarine blue. The pupils, lashes and eyebrows are Payne's grey. The iris is burnt umber with a white highlight.

The dress is painted with vermilion red. As this is a translucent colour it should be applied liberally and may need two coats. The petals of the flowers are cadmium yellow with a small amount of white added to give the colour opacity. The centres are dots of Payne's grey which is also used for the shadows.

THE FINISHED VERSION

In the finished version I made, I used the colour scheme I had worked out for the blue dress with white spots. The only difference in the treatment is that painting on the wood requires much more paint because of the ply's absorbency. I have added Payne's grey dots behind the white ones on the dress as shadows to give them depth.

Green and yellow dress

Green and red dress

Blue dress with white spots

Red dress with yellow flowers

Finished version

PROJECT 4

A ROOM WITH A VIEW. MEDITERRANEAN SCENE

In this composition I have used the device of putting a picture within a picture to give the illusion of space and depth. The walls, floor and furniture of the room frame open doors leading to a patio, which in turn surrounds a sea scape that is the focal point of the picture.

The room is painted in strong bright colours to give a cheerful and warm ambience. The table has a simple still life on it and I have emphasised pattern in the general decor to add interest to an uncomplicated interior.

This particular room and the view within it are entirely invented, many of the ingredients of the picture being drawn from previous works.

SCALING UP

To make the picture to the same scale as the original each square on the drawing represents 20 mm. This will give a finished picture 490 x 425 mm. including the frame. At this size some of the pieces are quite small and fiddly and you may wish to increase the scale to 30 or 40 mm. to make them more easily handled.

Materials

Birch ply: 6 mm. x 400 x 330
MDF: 6 mm. x 450 x 380
Birch ply offcuts: 4 mm. & 6 mm.
Planed softwood (knot free):
   25 mm. x 50 mm. x 2000 mm.

Wood glue, paste
Paints comprising titanium white, Payne's grey, cadmium yellow, lemon yellow, vermilion, crimson, ultramarine blue, Hooker's green, raw sienna, burnt sienna, burnt umber.

Scale drawing of project

THE FRAME

For this kind of picture with an integral painted frame, in a reversal of the normal procedure, I make the frame first.

The frame is cut from the softwood with its internal dimensions an exact match to the 6 mm. ply which forms the picture. The corners are mitred, preferably with a mitre saw. The 6 mm. ply is placed on the MDF and centred. A line is drawn around the ply on to the MDF and the ply removed. Glue is then applied to the MDF on the outside of the line and to the mitred corners of the softwood frame. The frame is now positioned on the MDF and cramped or put under pressure using the string and dowel method described in Chapter 5. Remember to protect the corners with corrugated card or the cord will crush the softwood.

As you tighten the cord up, the 6 mm. ply can be used as a template to make sure everything remains square. Put some weights on top of the frame to stick it firmly to the MDF. It is also helpful to slip some scraps of 6 mm. next to the MDF to support the frame where it overlaps the backing board. Leave it to dry overnight.

CUTTING OUT

The design can now be transferred to the 6 mm. ply and cut out on the fret saw. If you are working to the same scale as my original there should be no problems cutting it out as the picture is quite small. The one thing to bear in mind is that small fiddly bits, such as the pieces under the table, should be cut out early on while there is plenty of wood to hold on to and manoeuvre.

If you wish to simplify some of the cutting out process the floor tiles should be sawn in strips across the grain. The cuts with the grain are made through the top layer of the laminate using a knife to take out a 'v' section. This leaves easily identifiable strips rather than lots of squares.

In this picture there are no areas where wood is removed completely to reveal collage stuck to the background. You can therefore make the piece of ply that forms the sky thinner in order to create an extra level. Do this by splitting off two layers of laminate from the back using a chisel and sanding off the odd splinters that remain. This is quite easy, as the glue joints are a weak point, and leave you with a piece of ply 4 mm. thick.

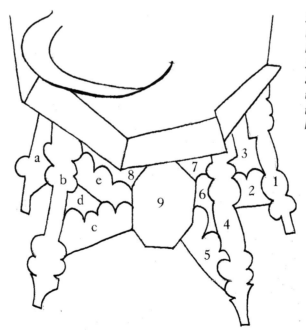

Suggested sequence for cutting up the table legs. a–e should be cut first followed by 1–9. Similar methods should be adopted in other places where there are small pieces such as the wine, the guitar and the boat.

BLOCKING UP

Starting from the centre, the balustrade, bottom leaf of the plant and its pot are blocked up with 4 mm. as are the back legs of the chair, the underneath of the table, the left-hand door and the curtain.

The table top, the top of the guitar, the right-hand door, the inside of the chair back and its front legs are blocked up with 6 mm.

The rest of the chair, the door knob, the wine, the glass and the rest of the guitar are blocked up by 10 mm. Do this by adding 4 mm. ply to the 6 mm. On the chair the 6 mm. goes under all but the back legs. Then the 4 mm. is added. This has a hole cut in it for the inside of the chair back to drop in to. The 6 mm. on the table top is run under the wine, the glass and the guitar. In the case of the guitar a hole should be cut in the 4 mm. blocking up material to create the sound box. The fret board should be shaved back at an angle so that it slants back to meet the top of the guitar which is 4 mm. lower than the sound box.

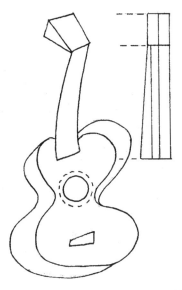

Detail of blocking up guitar. The dotted line round the sound box indicates the size of the hole made in the 4 mm. blocking up layer. The section on the right shows how the fretboard is shaved back to meet the top.

WHITTLING

The general rule applies that the edges of things furthest from the viewer are carved back the hardest. For example the outside edges of the sides of the guitar are carved back hard, as are the door frame, the balustrade on the top edge, the back of the chair seat and the back and bottom edges of the table.

The curtain edges should be well carved to give the folds roundness. Everything else should at least have a bevel on it except for the edges that butt up to the frame.

Shaping with the knife

Gluing up

GLUING UP

The picture is assembled and the thinnest pieces such as the sky glued first. The gluing happens in conjunction with the painting, the main washes of colour being applied first.

PAINTING

The frame is painted first so that the inside edge can be done easily before any of the picture is put in place. I gave it a thick coat of burnt umber followed, when dry, with a strong glaze of ultramarine. When this was dry I added spots of burnt sienna using a no. 12 point.

The sea and sky are painted with a wash of ultramarine. The sky is painted with a more diluted mixture. The clouds, sails of the boats and the balustrade are painted with titanium white. The foreground boat is painted with raw sienna followed by a strong mix of Payne's grey on the figures and in the shadow areas. Grey is also used in a light glaze on the centre parts of the component pieces of the balustrade.

The awning is painted with stripes of vermilion and white. The dado rail and the doors are painted cadmium yellow with a grey glaze on the shadow areas and white for highlights. The door knob is burnt umber with a yellow highlight.

The floor tiles are painted with a pink mixed from white and crimson. When making a pale tint like this it is best to add small amounts of the colour to the white as the white will be by far the largest ingredient. If you do it the other way round you are almost certain to end up with too much paint.

When the pink is dry, dots of vermilion are added with a fine sable point. The shadow of the balustrade and the edges of the tiles are painted with a glaze of grey.

The plant pot is vermilion with grey shadows and white highlights. The plant is an equal mix of Hooker's green and cadmium yellow with yellow highlights.

The curtains are painted vermilion with a hint of white. The pattern is added with the leftovers of the colours used for the rest of the picture. Although it looks quite complex it is not difficult to paint. The main thing is to stagger the pattern from one strip to the next to emphasise the folds. A glaze of grey is used for the shadows.

The floor is painted with an equal mix of ultramarine and white. Blobs of vermilion with just a hint of white are added with a fine sable point when the blue is dry.

The walls below the dado rail are

Painting the individual parts

painted with Hooker's green. Spots of the blue used for the floor are applied with a sable point, along with blobs of the green with a little white added. This green is used to paint the walls above the dado. Spots of green with more white mixed in are painted on together with dots of lemon yellow. This light green is used to paint the ceiling and the two strips that make the door frame. Lemon yellow dots are added to these.

The legs and arm fronts of the chair are given a wash of raw sienna followed by a thin glaze of burnt umber in their centres. The uphol-stery is painted pink made from a mixture of crimson and white. When dry, stripes of vermilion with a hint of white in it are painted on followed by white highlights and grey shadows.

The rug has its fringes and a set of triangles on the middle strip painted pink, mixed from crimson and white. The other set of triangles are Hooker's green with a little white added. The outer and centre patterns are crimson and lemon yellow. There are vermilion squares in the middle of the crimson and cadmium yellow ones in the middle of the lemon.

The table is burnt sienna. The guitar is raw sienna. Both have cadmium yellow and white highlights and grey shadows. A strong mix of grey is used for the guitar fretboard. A piece of collage can be stuck behind the soundbox of the guitar. I used a print of a head of Rembrandt as it was just the right size and the colours blended well.

The wine bottle is painted with Hooker's green with a crimson glaze for the wine. Crimson is used for the wine in the glass. The label, glass and bottle highlights are white with detail and shadow added in grey.

The painting is now complete and the picture can be varnished.

PROJECT 5

LANDSCAPE

The basic scene of this project does exist in the real world. There is the hill with the school buildings and the allotments in front of them. I can view it from a high position. However, amongst other things, I have imported objects such as the garden shed and changed the crops in the fields. I have combined viewpoints making it possible to see things which would otherwise be hidden.

As the picture developed I became very interested in the variety of patterns and textures contained within it and each time I made a new version I emphasised these aspects further. If this process was continued the figurative aspect of the picture would eventually disappear leaving an abstract painting.

The landscape is made as a low relief cut from 6 mm. ply with only minimal blocking up from 4 mm. material.

Materials

FOR THE LANDSCAPE
Birch ply: 6 mm. **x** 590 **x** 560
MDF: 6 mm. **x** 590 **x** 560
    for just the landscape or
       6 mm. **x** 920 **x** 645
    for the version with window
    and curtains.
Hardboard or other material for
blocking up:
       4 mm. **x** 400 **x** 600

**FOR THE WINDOW FRAME, PELMET
AND LEDGE**
Softwood: 15 mm. **x** 20 **x** 2500
         12 mm. **x** 12 **x** 1200
         12 mm. **x** 45 **x** 1600
         12 mm. **x** 15 **x** 1900
         12 mm. **x** 60 **x** 900
         12 mm. **x** 20 **x** 260
(Select softwood that is knot free).
Hardwood quadrant: 6 mm. **x** 920

FOR THE CURTAINS
Birch ply: 6 mm. **x** 620 **x** 150 (2 off)
         6 mm. **x** 630 **x** 250

VASE AND PICTURE FRAME
Oak version:
    Oak: 30 mm. **x** 230 **x** 220
MDF version:
    MDF: 18 mm. **x** 230 **x** 220
    and eggshells.
Birch ply: 6 mm. **x** 400 **x** 160
  and a picture.

GENERAL
Wood glue, collage material, paste.
Paints comprising titanium white,
Payne's grey, crimson, vermilion red,
cadmium yellow, ultramarine blue,
olive green, Hooker's green, raw
sienna, burnt umber.

SCALING UP
To make the picture on the same
scale as the materials' specification
each square represents 3 cm. If you
want to use a jigsaw to cut this
design you will need to double the
scale at least, making each square
6 cm. and increasing the materials
accordingly.

Working drawing

Scale drawing of landscape

*Scale drawing of window frame,
curtains, vase and picture.*

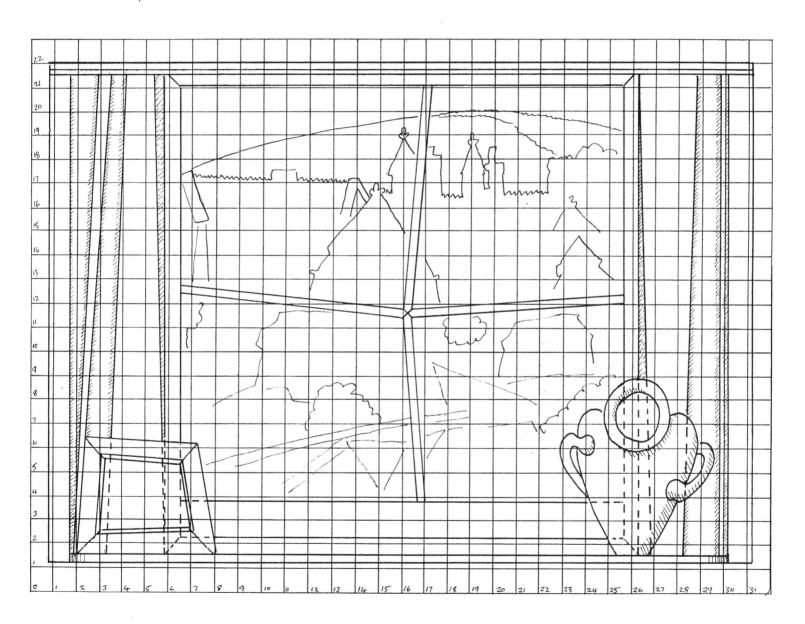

CUTTING OUT THE LANDSCAPE

If you are scaling the project up to 3 cm. and like me have a fret saw with only a 14 inch throat you will need to make a series of cuts from both sides of the board.

First saw the board in half along the top of the middle wall. This is marked no. 1 on the illustration. Start cutting on the left-hand side wiggling round the top of the tree. It is then a relatively straight run and the cut will get almost to the next tree before the back of the throat is reached. The wood is now withdrawn and cutting started again from the right-hand side. It weaves round some foliage, along the top of the shed roof, on to the wall, from there to the tree in the middle and over that to meet the cut from the other direction.

Next remove the sky, marked 2 on the illustration. Again cutting from the left side first, going up the curve of the hill. Then saw in from the right moving the wood in a see-saw motion to create a ripple in the cut for the trees on the hillside.

The piece below is now cut up the right-hand side of the left chimney stack and through the hedgerow to the top of the hill, making two pieces small enough to be manipulated easily in the saw. This is cut no. 3 on the illustration.

The sequence of cuts to divide the picture in to easily managed pieces on the fret saw.

The bottom piece is slightly more difficult as there is no easy centre cut and it is best approached by reducing it in size. The simple shapes of the building at the bottom are cut off first. Then saw away the foliage on the right-hand side. Remove as large sections as possible, leaving the detail cuts until later.

Cut out the road sign and the tree behind it, this will enable you to saw along the top of the wall. The way is now clear to cut down the wall to the left of the tree, along to the right-hand side of the greenhouse, down it and around the left-hand side of the bath. This is cut no. 4 on the illustration. The remaining pieces are now easily sawn.

As this is a complex picture with many tiny bits, it is best to re-assemble them on a board as they are cut.

Try to cut the fine detail and intricate pieces whilst the small bits are still attached to the large ones. Saw out all the window panes while the frame is still joined to the surrounding wall. Do the zigzag cuts on the ridge tiles before the straight cuts so that there is plenty of wood to hold on to and control while sawing.

The greenhouse can be sawn out without using piercing cuts to remove the panes. One possible pattern is shown below.

The prime consideration with something that has as many pieces to be removed as this is to try to cut three sides of each panel as progress is made along the route. Then, on the return journey, as bits are removed and the remaining framework becomes increasingly frail, the number of cuts left to be made are at a minimum.

This shows one possible route to saw out the greenhouse without the use of piercing cuts. The dotted lines indicate where the cuts pass through the framework.

I find it easier when cutting intricate work on thin wood such as this, to use a blade that has lost its first keenness. A brand new blade saws the wood too fast and it is easy to overshoot a tight corner. The slightly dull blade cuts just that bit slower and is more controllable. It is in this situation that having a variable speed control on the saw would be very helpful.

Do not feel it is necessary to cut every line shown in the drawing. For example, I sawed the cloches out in one piece and then carved the detail in with a knife.

CARVING THE LANDSCAPE

Generally when dealing with a low relief such as this one, the subject matter will determine how it is to be carved. Where something is receding from the viewer, the further away it gets, the more wood that is removed. A simple illustration of this is a roof. The gutter edge, presuming it to be nearest the eye has little or nothing removed. All the carving is concentrated on the top. If the roof is coming towards the viewer, then all the carving happens on top and at the back. The top back corner has the most wood removed, the back being the part of the roof furthest from the eye.

The same rule applies to the walls. Because of the high viewpoint chosen for this picture the base of the walls is furthest away and therefore has the most wood removed.

All the pieces should have a slight bevel, cut or sanded off every side, except where they are at the edge of the picture.

Foliage should have its edges well rounded. Where one tree or shrub comes in front of another the one behind should have its overlapped edge carved well back. For 6 mm. ply I would cut in to two laminates or more so that the contour lines are well exposed.

If the greenhouse is cut out avoiding the use of piercing cuts it is too frail to do much with apart from carving out the thick edge at the bottom. Here a good bevel can be cut around the tree and along the ground.

Account does need to be taken, when carving, as to whether a piece is going to be blocked up or not. If it is to be blocked up, by how much? As this is a low relief the chances are that most pieces will have a difference in height of 4 mm. or less. Where this is so, if the work is not carved too deeply the blocking up material is not seen and does not need to be cut so accurately.

All of the landscape can be carved with a knife. However I used a medium sized gouge for the sky. I wanted to carve it at a shallow angle in order to reveal the contour lines of the ply as fairly widely spaced. On a reasonably large piece of wood such as this it is easier to use a gouge. The work is held firmly by clamping it to a bench with a 'G' clamp and then small shavings removed with a gouge and mallet.

Carving the sky with a shallow gouge to reveal the contour lines in the ply. Remember to keep the cuts diagonal to the grain.

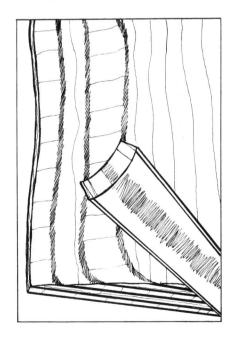

LOCATING THE LANDSCAPE ON THE BACKING BOARD

This section is only relevant if you are making the version with the window frame and curtains.

Draw a line along the MDF backing board 10 mm. in from the top edge. Do the same at the bottom. Draw two vertical lines 150 mm. in from either side. Within this rectangle draw a line 15 mm. in from the top and two side lines. Draw a line 45 mm. up from the bottom line. This inner rectangle defines the landscape area.

Assemble the landscape pieces within the rectangle. A frame is now made around the landscape using a strip of 12 x 15 mm. softwood 560 mm. long either side and 620 mm. long across the top. A piece of 12 x 45 mm. softwood 620 mm. long goes along the bottom. This piece will form the window sill. The inside edges of these pieces should be painted white before they are glued in to position.

BLOCKING UP

It is perfectly acceptable to rely on just the carving and paint finish for the low relief effect. However it can be enhanced by blocking up parts of the picture with thin material.

In the version I made I used 4 mm. hardboard as outlined below.

The sky and hillside are not raised at all. On the buildings below, starting with the left-hand side, the left end wall and the dressed stone are blocked up, as are the roofs and stone lips of the gables, the turret, the buttresses, and the right end wall.

In the centre, the entire gable end, the roof to the front of the chimney, the chimney stack and the turret are raised, but not the ridge or the right-hand section of roof.

On the right, the roofs, turret, chimney stack and the gable ends are raised but not the ridge, the walls either side of the chimney or the door. The trees on the right next to the gable are also blocked up.

Below this, the dressed stone top of the wall is raised, as are the greenhouse, the water butt, the foliage of the apple trees and the shed apart from its door and foundations. Also in the allotments the cloches, the gardeners, the compost pile, and the top of the bath are blocked up.

The shading indicates the parts of the picture that are blocked up with the 4 mm.

In the foreground, the dressed stone top of the two walls are raised along with the road sign, as are the barge boards, roofs, chimney of the building and all the foliage on the right.

Any of the pieces of blocking up material that raise more than one piece of the picture should be glued to the backing board provided they can be located accurately. None of the picture should be glued until at least the shadows and local colour are painted.

The window frame construction

Cut the 20 x 15 mm. in to four equal lengths. These should be mitred at each end with their longest length being 620 mm.

Glue the corners and put them under pressure with a cord and dowel using the method described in Chapter 5. Check that it is square, then leave it until the glue is dry, preferably overnight.

THE GLAZING BARS
Cut four pieces of 12 x 12 mm. softwood 350 mm. long with a mitre cut on one end. Mitre this end again from the other side to create a point.

Place the full scale drawing on a flat surface and arrange the four pieces of wood on the drawing to create an interesting division of the picture. Avoid cutting figures in half or destroying the sense of an object. If the joints are not perfect, adjust the angles to fit. This is easily done with a sharp knife.

An option at this point is to bevel the edges of the glazing bars. I did all four sides of each one with a block plane, making the wood octagonal in cross section. This has the advantages of making the bars look lighter and obscuring less of the picture underneath.

Now position the previously glued window frame over the glazing bars, lining it up with the edges of the picture underneath. Mark where the glazing bars come on the frame and where they need to be cut to fit. Cut them one by one, on the outside of the cutting line so that they are a tight fit. Place some scraps of 4 mm. ply underneath them to rebate them slightly in the frame and then glue them in position. Rebating them gives some extra clearance from the picture below to allow for blocking up.

If you have cut them correctly, their own tightness should be enough

to hold them while the glue goes off. However if pressure is required some can be exerted with the cord and dowel. This is set up round the frame as before with the addition of blocks of scrap on the outside of the frame opposite the ends of the glazing bars. When the cord is tightened it will put some pressure on the scrap blocks and tend to push the frame in at those points.

THE WINDOW LEDGE, CURTAINS AND PELMET
The window frame is now located on top of the picture frame on the base board. Then a strip of 20 x 20 mm. softwood 620 mm. long is glued either side. This will be rebated in from the base board edge by 10 mm. at the top and bottom as marked previously. Two more pieces of 20 x 20 mm. softwood are glued flush with the right and left edges of the base board. These are 630 mm. long and are only rebated 10 mm. from the top edge as they come flush at the bottom. The four pieces of wood form the supports for the curtains.

The window ledge can now be located. This is made from a piece of softwood 12 x 60 x 880 mm. The ends of this have the front corners cut in a curve and the edges rounded off.

It is positioned between the two longer pieces of 20 x 20 mm. softwood at either end of the background and glued to the bottom of the window frame. Care should be taken not to glue it to anything else at this point as the window ledge and frame need to be detachable until painting is completed.

The curtains are made from two birch ply panels 620 x 150 x 6 mm. These are glued on to the 20 mm. strips so that they fit neatly either side of the window frame. The other piece of ply is cut in to strips as illustrated. These are whittled and sanded along their length and placed to produce the folds in the curtains. Strips 630 mm. long are placed at either end so that the curtains fall either side of the window ledge. Some small scraps of 6 mm. ply are stuck on the bottom of the 20 mm. softwood to fill in the gaps.

A pelmet is cut to run along the picture from end to end. It is made from a piece of 12 x 45 mm. softwood 920 mm. long with a length of 6 mm. quadrant stuck under the front edge. It should not be attached until it and the curtains are painted.

The oak version, cut and carved

The vase

OAK VERSION

This is cut on the fretsaw with two piercing cuts forming the handles. I used a no. 9 blade and cut very slowly. It could also be cut with a jigsaw.

It needs to be clamped firmly for carving. I pinched it securely with the four plastic jaws on the Workmate.

The wood from the back of the handles is removed first with a shallow gouge. The piece is then turned over. The bulk of the carving on the front is also done with a shallow gouge. The carving should reflect the tapering shape with more wood being removed at the bottom and shoulders.

The rim at the top is made by hollowing out the middle. A gouge with the same or a slightly smaller radius than the circle should be used. A scoring cut is made all round to prevent splitting. Then the wood is removed starting on cuts with the grain, from the top and bottom and then working round. The last cuts of each sequence always being the ones across the grain. The deepest part of the curved hole should be towards the body of the vase.

The outside of the rim is made in the same way except that a gouge with a slightly larger radius than the circle is used. Alternatively it can be done with a parting tool or a veiner. The wood can either be left with a carved finish or sanded smooth.

MDF VERSION

In this rendition the handles are cut as separate pieces. The rim is also separated from the main body of the vase. The centre is removed from the rim using a piercing cut and, using it as a template, a replacement is made from 6 mm. material.

As the MDF is soft all the carving can be done with a knife. A bevel with a fairly gentle radius is put on all edges that face the front. The main body of the vase is tapered and rounded towards the bottom and on the shoulders. All the carving is sanded smooth and the eggshell applied. Be careful not to glue eggshells in any of the joints.

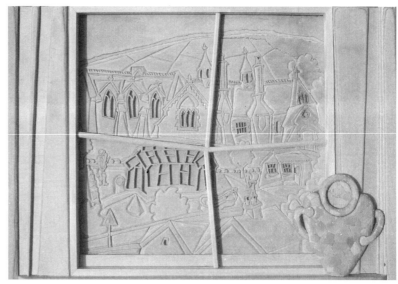

The MDF version, cut and carved

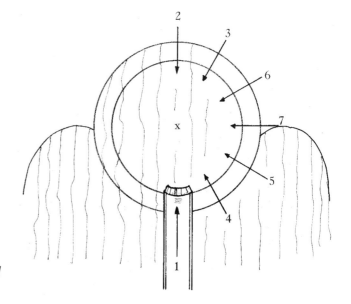

Sequence of cuts with the gouge to hollow out the top of the oak vase. All cuts finish at the centre and they should be repeated on the left side.

THE PICTURE FRAME

This is made from 6 mm. birch ply. First a picture is chosen and two strips of ply placed either side of it, overlapping the edges. Then two more are placed, one at the top and the other at the bottom. Their ends should overlap the side pieces. All four are moved until they frame the picture in a pleasing fashion.

Then the four pieces are taped together securely with masking tape and diagonals drawn in the corners where they overlap. These diagonals are cut through on the saw. When a cut is made it should be re-taped until all four cuts are done. This will produce a perfectly fitted mitre joint even though the frame is not necessarily a rectangle.

The four pieces are now reassembled on another piece of 6 mm. ply and drawn around to produce a backing board. This can be cut smaller if desired.

The edges of the frame are now given a bevel using a knife and sandpaper.

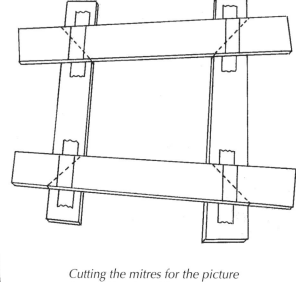

Cutting the mitres for the picture frame. The dotted lines above indicate the saw cuts.

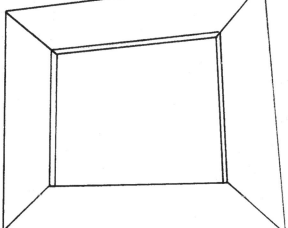

Painting technique

As this picture is a compilation of various drawings and photographs made on different days and from different places I felt it was worth while to produce a colour rough.

The rough is made up in several pieces. The landscape is painted on a sheet of water-colour paper. The window frame is cut from a piece of thin card, as are the curtains, small picture frame and vase. This gives some flexibility in trying out different arrangements.

The scheme outlined below may at first seem rather complex, but this is only because of the large number of objects to be painted. Many of the pieces are treated in a similar fashion and there are a number of constants. The main ones are the use of Payne's grey as the shadow colour and raw sienna as the background for stone and brickwork.

THE COLOUR ROUGH
(see colour illustration on p. 91)

The three strips of shadow, one on the hills and two on the walls are painted quite heavily. This creates bands of light and dark colour helping to give depth to the picture.

Although the windows in the final picture are collage, if you prefer an all painted finish Payne's grey, ultramarine and white are a good solution. The grey-blue colour combination is recessive, hinting at the depth of the rooms behind the windows, while the white suggests the light catching the glass.

THE SKY
The sky is painted with a wash of ultramarine blue which is allowed to dry, then the titanium white clouds are added. If you wish the clouds to be more diffused paint them while the blue is still damp or add water round their edges. If a warmer feel is wanted add a little yellow to the clouds while the white is still wet and blend it in. For a cooler effect use Payne's grey. If you want the clouds to appear denser, use the grey to make shadow areas and the yellow to create highlights.

THE HILLSIDE
The woodland is olive green with spots of Hooker's green on top to suggest the texture of the trees. The yellow field is cadmium. The green fields are a mixture of cadmium yellow and olive green with olive green field boundaries and blobs of titanium white for the sheep. The ploughed fields are raw sienna with burnt umber furrows. The shadow is a glaze of Payne's grey which is also run along the field divisions overlapping the green.

Shadow areas painted

The buildings and walls

The roofs and turrets are painted with a wash of Payne's grey which is followed by a thicker application of the same colour to delineate the shadow areas and the gutters. The slates are a mixture of Payne's grey and titanium white dabbed on.

The stonework is a wash of raw sienna, followed by a wash of Payne's grey. The stones are painted on with a thin mix of burnt umber with a little white. More white is added to this mixture to paint the areas of dressed stone.

The windows are a combination of Payne's grey and ultramarine.

The brick wall is painted with a wash of raw sienna followed by a glaze of Payne's grey which extends as far as the coping stones. These are treated in the same way as the dressed stones above. The bricks are painted in with crimson.

The allotment

The frame of the greenhouse is painted white with grey shadows. There is also a hint of burnt umber in the panel. The greenhouse glass and the cold frames are ultramarine with Payne's grey shadows and titanium white highlights, as is the water in the drum and the bath. The drum and the bottom of the bath are crimson.

The trees are painted with olive green, yellow being added for the highlights and grey or Hooker's green for the shadow areas. The apples are crimson with a blob of yellow on top. They may need more than one coat or a little white added for opacity. The trunks of the trees are burnt umber with raw sienna highlights and Payne's grey shadows, as is the compost heap.

The shed is painted with a wash of raw sienna for the wooden part, with grey for the shadows and the foundation. The corrugated iron roof is stripes of grey, blue and white and the same colours are used for the windows.

The paths are a wash of raw sienna with dots of grey, brown, yellow and white. The garden plots are painted variously with the olive green and yellow mixture or burnt umber and raw sienna. Dots, lines, blobs and squiggles of any of the other colours are added to simulate broken earth and rows of vegetables. Much the same treatment is given to the two gardeners, making them predominantly brown and spotty as though dressed in tweed.

The foreground

The wall in the foreground has the same treatment as the stonework above with a grey wash for shadow. The roof and chimney stack of the building have a wash of raw sienna. The tiles and bricks are painted crimson and the roof is then given a glaze of burnt umber which is also used for the right-hand wall. The barge boards are Payne's grey applied thickly, with a thin wash of the same applied as a shadow over the gables. Lines of burnt umber are added to indicate planking.

The road sign is vermilion with a white background and grey applied thickly for the exclamation mark. The trees have the same treatment as the ones above.

The window frame, curtains and ornaments

The window frame is white with a grey shadow. The shadows for the inside of the room do not quite agree with what is going on outside, but are painted to emphasise the idea that light is coming in through the window.

The curtains are a wash of vermilion with grey shadows added. Then a simple pattern of flowers with white petals and yellow centres is painted on using a 10 mm. flat brush.

The vase is cadmium yellow with a grey shadow. The colours are applied quite strongly.

The picture is a piece of collage made from two photographs of Picasso. The frame is painted with a wash of burnt umber, grey shadows and yellow highlights. A grain pattern is added to the wood using a thicker mix of the burnt umber applied with a small sable point.

Painting the finished version
(see colour illustrations on p. 91)

I have largely followed the colour scheme worked out in the rough, there are however a few changes and additions.

THE LANDSCAPE
All the shadow areas on the land-scape are painted first using grey. The roofs of the school buildings also get a coat of grey, the shadows being defined by a denser layer of paint.

Next the local or background colour is added.

THE SKY
The clouds in the sky are painted on the blue after it is dry. They are painted first with white using a sable point. I used a no. 4 with very long hair. The paint is blobbed on fairly freely with the densest part of the clouds receiving several coats. When they are sufficiently strong a very small amount of yellow is added to the white and this is dotted on the edges facing the light source, to give the effect of sunlit clouds.

THE HILLSIDE
The fields are treated in the same way as the colour rough, although I have changed the layout slightly. For the furrows, rather than making uniform stripes I have bent them around to give a bit of contour to the hillside. For this I used a no. 2 sable point and overpainted the burnt umber of the furrows, one field with vermilion, one with yellow and one with a mixture of the two. This gives them depth and emphasises the design.

Two of the yellow fields have spots on them of yellow with a hint of burnt umber. This together with the white dots of the sheep and the brown blobs for cows adds to the patchwork pattern of the hillside.

THE BUILDINGS
These are also treated as the colour rough except that I have varied the colour mixtures slightly. When the rows of blobs are painted on to represent roof tiles the mix is varied by the addition of small amounts of grey or white so the tiles are not uniform.

For the dressed stone white and yellow are applied quite thickly, wet in to wet, in the highlight areas. The rest of the stone is painted with burnt umber, yellow and white, and again the mix is frequently adjusted very slightly to give variation to the colour.

For the brick wall in front I have substituted vermilion for crimson, because of its extra brightness glowing out of the dark shadow. The bricks are painted on with the no. 2 sable point, applying the paint thickly. Because the red paint is quite translucent you may find it easier to paint the bricks before the shadow is added.

THE ALLOTMENT
In the allotment I have brightened the colour and pattern considerably to convey the vibrancy of a flower filled garden. By contrast I have made the gardeners more subdued by leaving them largely burnt umber.

The background patchwork of plots is made of washes of raw sienna or yellow with a hint of olive green here and there. Then dots and lines of colour are added in profusion.

I have also enlivened the trees by dotting on the paint and using a small amount of white in the mixes together with the yellow.

THE FOREGROUND
This has been left largely the same except that the foliage is treated as above and the gable ends are painted more simply. They have a wash of Payne's grey followed when dry by stripes of white.

THE WINDOW FRAME
As in the colour rough, the frame, sill, ledge, pelmet and a thin strip either side of the window are painted white. As it is a relatively large area of flat colour I used acrylic primer-undercoat and gave it two coats, sanding with 120 grit paper in between.

The shadow on it is painted with Payne's grey. I found it easier to apply the paint with a J-Cloth. A corner of the cloth is dipped in the thinned colour and then rubbed on to the surface. The colour goes on flat and it is easy to run along the edges, keeping them neat. Any paint that does go over an edge can be wiped off with a clean damp cloth.

The shadow is applied to the fronts of the window frame, glazing bars, window ledge and pelmet. It is also applied to the top of the pelmet, the bottom of the window ledge and the two strips of white either side of the window.

THE CURTAINS
For the finished picture I decided on a geometric pattern, reflecting the many triangles in the landscape.

The shadows on the curtains are painted in quite darkly with Payne's grey and their edges softened by running a brush filled with water along them. This is followed with a wash of vermilion.

When this is dry the pattern is mapped out with cadmium yellow. Use as large a brush as you can. A 10 mm. flat or a number 12 round is a good size. Make each line with one stroke getting it about 5 mm. wide. Don't make the pattern too precisely. Make sure it doesn't match properly where it transfers from one piece of wood to the next, in order to empha-sise the folds.

All the downward pointing trian-gles now have a smaller triangle painted inside them in olive green. All the upward pointing triangles have a smaller triangle painted in them with vermilion. If the green triangles seem too strong they can be knocked back with a glaze of yellow. If the red triangles are too weak they can be strengthened with the addi-tion of a little white.

If the curtains seem too bright in comparison to the rest of the picture give the shadow areas another coat of Payne's grey.

THE VASE
For the oak version the shadows are added with grey and the wood either varnished, polished or oiled.

For the eggshell version all the pieces are given a coat of Payne's grey. The paint is worked well in to all the cracks. It is allowed to dry and then sanded down thoroughly with 120 grit paper.

The shadows are painted in with grey and allowed to dry. At this point the pieces can be glued together. They should be a good enough fit that glue in the joints will suffice. Place the vase on a sheet of paper while it is gluing so that it cannot stick to the bench.

The whole surface is now given a strong glaze of ultramarine. I did this with two coats, lightly sanding the left-hand side in between to produce a gentle highlight.

THE COLLAGE
Most of the windows in the buildings are so small that any brightly col-oured pictures will do.

For the three windows on the left

it is worth being more selective. I used a small picture of some stained glass and bits of a reproduction of an early Victorian painting. This is an interior scene with figures and windows in it that give depth to the room.

Pictures of paintings are often a good source of material for collage, particularly for small areas, as they often have better definition than ordinary photographs.

I glued some chrome foil in the hole in the drum next to the greenhouse to simulate reflecting water. I had originally planned to use a piece of a CD that I had cut up on the fret saw but the foil was thinner and therefore more suitable.

For the greenhouse I first glued in a background picture of flowers to cover the interior. Over this at the left-hand end I added part of a picture of a conservatory. On the right-hand side I put in a garden view down a rose arbour. Both these pictures have strong perspective and give the greenhouse depth. In the middle I have put in some jungle with tropical birds to add colour, some pumpkins and cactus to add diversity and a gardener to populate it.

This is a fairly conservative solution. It could have a party happening in it or anything else that takes your fancy. Go through magazines and try placing the greenhouse over pictures to see how they look. Use the greenhouse as a template and cut the pictures out and combine them. You are bound to come up with something interesting.

Final assembly

With all the painting and the collage completed the landscape can now be glued down. Start with it assembled and work from the top down, taking out the pieces in strips, gluing them and replacing them. Where pieces are blocked up glue the lower bits that surround them first. Do not use too much glue, particularly on pieces such as window frames and remove any surplus with a damp cloth.

Varnish makes a good adhesive and for something like the greenhouse with its delicate structure and complex shape it is worth leaving it until the varnish is applied. The background can be given a coat, the greenhouse pressed in to the wet paint and then varnished. This will be sufficient to fix it firmly in place.

When the glue is dry the landscape is varnished. I used a satin finish applied with an 18 mm. brush. Do not varnish the frame where the window is glued as it will inhibit the glue's strength.

The curtains and the window frame can also be varnished now and this will enable you to paint the back of the glazing bars easily.

When everything is dry the frame can be glued in place as can the picture and vase either side of it.

My final version

After some thought I chose the eggshell finish vase for the final picture. I felt it needed the strength of colour to compete with the rest of the composition. It is also good to have the contrast of a completely different material. This is one of the reasons I use eggshell so much in my work.

I then sat and contemplated the picture for some time. Eventually and somewhat reluctantly I decided that the glazing bars had to go. They helped considerably to create the effect of a view through a window. Unfortunately, as far as I was concerned, they fragmented the landscape too much. The landscape needed to be simpler or designed to divide naturally in to four panels.

I gently broke the glazing bars out, sanded the glue off, patched up the white where they had been and varnished it.

I hung it on the wall, sat down and took another long look at it. Had I made the right decision?

Colour rough (see p. 86)

Greenhouse collage detail

Completed version with glazing bars

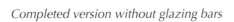

Completed version without glazing bars

Project 1 (see p. 46)
Desert Island

Project 2 (see p. 51)
Still Life: Fruit & Wine on a Tray

GALLERY OF WORK

Still life on a cabriole table 56 x 87 cm.
The objects on the table of this still life are made from birch ply.
The jug is built up from four layers of 6 mm. ply which were
carved and sanded back to give it form. A grid was used to distort
the picture in the book to fit the page. The cabriole legs are
marine ply with a thick yew veneer glued on top.

Guitar and wine 142 x 78 cm.
This relief was cut out entirely using a jig saw and most of the
shaping was done with a router and a half-round profile
cutter. Hence it is fairly bold and simple. The piece can be
leaned against a wall on its own legs or hung. It is constructed
in various woods including elm, ash and 18 and 9 mm. ply.
The guitar strings are fishing line, a print of the Mona Lisa is
glued in the soundbox and the sheet music is painted paper.

The Charlton Arms at Ludford 126 x 88 cm.
This large landscape was created from a series of sketches from different viewpoints combined with a number of photographs. I was particularly interested in the zigzag construction of the bridge and this part of the picture alone is made from several different positions.
Because it is large it was made in a number of different sections and is predominantly 6 mm. birch ply with some 9 mm. mounted on a 6 mm. MDF background and 25 mm. soft wood for the capstones on the bridge.
It is painted with acrylics and there is collage behind all the windows.

Fishing boats, Lossiemouth 61 x 52 cm.
A relief cut from one sheet of ply and using an integral frame.
Note the use of a piece of string for a mooring rope in the bottom right-hand corner. I stiffened the string and generated a curve in it by dipping it in varnish and hanging it up.

Sea stack No. 1 Gowies castle 66 x 61 cm.

This is the first of a series of pictures I have made of sea stacks on the coast of the Moray Firth in northern Scotland. This one is a fairly literal interpretation of the subject.

I have used a variety of different woods to make the sea stack including oak, pitch pine and birch ply. The beach is done in eggshell with small pieces of drift wood collected from near the actual sea stack glued to it. The sea and sunset are painted on a linen canvas that was stuck on behind the stack. I wetted the linen before gluing so that it would shrink as it dried and stretch tight.

Sea stack No. 3 82 x 63 x 9 cm.

I chose to make this version out of a variety of woods and to give it quite a lot of depth. The stack itself is made from beech and has been lightly carved. The jumble of rocks to the side and in front are a mixture of woods, but mostly oak. They are also all different in thickness and were very hard to fit together as I did not plan it thoroughly beforehand. The foreground is birch ply and the background is MDF. The whole thing is framed with a thin oak box.

White to mate in three moves 83 x 95 x 16 cm.
This picture is more three dimensional than most reliefs. The chess pieces are cut at an angle across their bases so that they stick out from the board generating their own shadows. They also have painted shadows which may or may not coincide with the real ones, depending on the lighting. The boards, table top and tea tray are also set at different angles to each other. It is constructed in birch ply and oak faced ply except for the table which is pine.
The chess pieces are laid out in a genuine problem.

Icon No. 2 34 x 38 x 9 cm.
In this version I have explored the use of several different finishes in conjunction with each other. The main part of the face is MDF painted crimson and then leafed with Dutch metal. I have made no attempt to patch up the leaf and have left it very ragged along the jaw line to allow the crimson to show through and to give the piece an antique feel.
The other part of the face is eggshelled as is part of the breast. I made the hair and the breast from 18 mm. birch ply and carved it deeply to reveal the contours of the laminates. The board behind the hair has a stipple effect.

Still life with Retsina 108 x 106 x 10 cm.
This large still life uses all three methods of relief construction. The background wall is MDF painted cream and rag rolled with a yellow glaze. The onions in the picture on it are made from 18 mm. birch ply that has been carved quite deeply to reveal the contours in the ply. This accentuates the layer effect of the onions. The table is made from pitch pine offcuts. The bowl of fruit is ply with the oranges being built up and carved back to make them round. The wine bottle and glass are birch ply. The label on the bottle is real as is the crown cap in front of it. I crushed the crown cap flat in a vice and stuck it to the table with a blob of silicone.

The trumpeter knows his onions
43 x 69 cm.
The trumpet is fret cut ply that has been covered in Dutch metal. The shadows and highlights have been painted on top of the metal with acrylics. The onions are also fret cut ply and the background is MDF covered in collage.

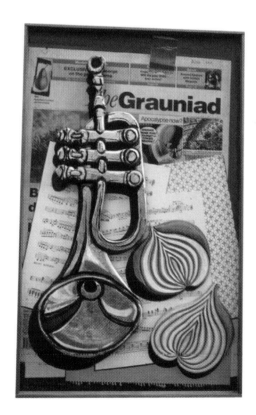

Gas Street Basin 92 x 76 cm.
This is a partially demolished building in
Birmingham next to the canal.
It is done in low relief and cut from one
sheet of birch ply. As Birmingham appar-
ently has more miles of canal than Venice
it seemed appropriate to use some collage
of Venice in the doorway where the canal
can be seen.

Stop worrying 46 x 72 x 6 cm.
In this picture I have used
a variety of materials to
create different textures.
The blue and white of the
sky were painted at the
same time so that the wet
colours would blend
together. The facade of the
main building is eggshelled
hardboard with birch ply
doors, windows, balus-
trades and pillars. The
pillars are Payne's grey
with flecks of gold added.
The road has old sandpa-
per glued to it to give the
tarmac texture and the
washing hanging from the
sign has photographs of
clothing stuck on it.

Mediterranean scene after Picasso 125 x 87 cm.
This picture is almost entirely a copy of a Picasso painting. It was
made after a holiday in Minorca and I have added a typical
Minorcan gate. The other alterations are in materials, method and
the introduction of mixed media. One central window has a small
convex mirror behind it. This has the effect of reflecting the
viewer, at about the right scale, as though they are in the picture.

Alpujarra village 62 x 45 cm.
The Alpujarra is a region high in the Sierra Nevada in southern Spain, where the villages cut steps in to the steep hillsides.
This is a relatively naturalistic rendition of part of a village done entirely in low relief on birch ply with collage behind the windows of the houses.

The yellow path 64 x 64 cm.
This is another picture like the previous one, cut from one sheet of ply and relying on carving to create the relief effect.
I have made everything curvaceous emphasising the roundness in the natural landscape.

A room with a view No. 5. Old Perithea, Corfu. 88 x 47 x 11 cm.
This picture harks back to project four again. A defining feature of this is that it is built around an old metal window frame that I had kept for many years, sure it would come in useful. It seemed perfect for a composition based on an old and mostly abandoned village and so I designed the view to fit it. The shrine in the corner contains a photograph of the interior of an actual shrine in the village.

Tower 46 x 62 cm.
The tower is created entirely from 6 mm. birch ply offcuts from previous works, stuck on to an MDF background. The offcuts are mostly the pieces removed from windows from a variety of works and only two or three of them were cut to fit. It was made without any preliminary drawings. I painted the background board and then placed the offcuts on it, moving them around until I felt they looked right. Then I painted the red lattice work on them and stuck them down. The rest of the colours were added when it was all assembled.

Desert moon 47 x 29 x 7 cm.
Another simple relief built up in layers. The moon is a pebble, the background desert is eggshelled and the spines on the cactus are panel pins. The picture is enclosed in a mitred frame that has been painted blue and then had a dark grey glaze dragged over it.